# SAY IT *ISN'T* SEW!

this book belongs to

_____

LEISURE ARTS, INC.
Little Rock, Arkansas

# SAY IT ISN'T SEW!

## EDITORIAL STAFF

*Vice President and Editor-in-Chief:* Sandra Graham Case
*Executive Director of Publications:* Cheryl Nodine Gunnells
*Special Projects Design Director:* Patricia Wallenfang Uhiren
*Senior Publications Designer:* Dana Vaughn
*Senior Director of Publications:* Susan White Sullivan
*Craft Publications Director:* Kristine Anderson Mertes
*Editorial Director:* Susan Frantz Wiles
*Senior Director of Public Relations and Retail Marketing:* Stephen Wilson
*Senior Art Operations Director:* Jeff Curtis

TECHNICAL —
*Technical Editor:* Leslie Schick Gorrell
*Senior Technical Writer:* Michelle James
*Production Assistant:* Shawnna B. Bowles
*Technical Associates:* Theresa Hicks Young
*Design Assistants:* Karla Edgar and Joyce Holland

EDITORIAL —
*Senior Editor:* Suzie Puckett
*Associate Editor:* Susan McManus Johnson

ART —
*Art Publications Director:* Rhonda Hodge Shelby
*Art Imaging Director:* Mark Hawkins
Graphic Artists: Karen Allbright, Shalana Frisby, and Dayle S. Carozza
*Imaging Technicians:* Stephanie Johnson and Mark R. Potter
*Imaging Assistants:* Steven L. Cooper and Sid Curtis
*Photography Coordinator:* Karen Hall
*Photostylists:* Janna Laughlin and Sondra Daniel
*Staff Photographers:* Lloyd L. Litsey and Andrew P. Uilkie
*Publishing Systems Administrator:* Becky Riddle
*Publishing Systems Assistants:* Clint Hanson, John Rose, and Chris Wertenberger

## BUSINESS STAFF

*Publisher:* Rick Barton.
*Vice President, Finance:* Tom Siebenmorgen
*Director of Corporate Planning and Development:* Laticia Mull Dittrich
*Vice President, Retail Marketing:* Bob Humphrey
*Vice President, Sales:* Ray Shelgosh
*Vice President, National Accounts:* Pam Stebbins
*Director of Sales and Services:* Margaret Reinold
*Vice President, Operations:* Jim Dittrich
*Comptroller, Operations:* Rob Thieme
*Retail Customer Service Manager:* Stan Raynor
*Print Production Manager:* Fred F. Pruss

Made in the United States of America

Softcover ISBN 1-57486-404-1

10 9 8 7 6 5 4 3 2 1

Be your own decorator without sewing a stitch? **Say it isn't so!** Yes, it is so with no-sew! This book will show you how to make beautiful home furnishings, such as pillows, window treatments, table toppers, even ottomans. And best of all … you don't need a sewing machine!

I'm sure you're already asking yourself, "What's the trick?" To find the answer, just plug in your iron and join me as I introduce you to the world of "fusibles" and glue. What IS a "fusible?" Fusible web bonds fabrics together without stitching. You simply iron the adhesive material onto your fabric, remove the paper backing, and then iron your two fabrics together. It's that easy!

So get ready to make it yourself, and create your own designer look that expresses your individual style! This book is filled with step-by-step instructions and tips to help you along the way…lampshades, chair cushions, baskets, and furniture. Yes, furniture! See the amazing makeover magic on a wingback chair, sofa table, buffet, and wardrobe cabinet. I hope you enjoy the photos of all the different home décor items you can make.

For inspiration, we've included seven different room themes — from a perky sunroom to a sophisticated bedroom. We also added decorating tips on fabric and trim selection to help you set the mood with color and pattern.

After mastering the simple no-sew techniques, you can create most of these projects in only an hour or two. Giving your home personality has never been easier. Before long, your friends will be begging you to share your no-sew secret!

So whether you want to freshen up your décor with a few new accents or tackle an entire room makeover, do it the easy stitchless way. "Say it ISN'T sew!" will be the response when you tell your guests you made it all yourself without a sewing machine.

*Patti Uhiren*

# contents

42

52

62

# contents

# tropical
## TREASURE

*Vacation in the tropics year round with these wonderfully exotic furnishings. Using our easy, no-sew techniques, it's a breeze to create this island oasis! Simply deck out bamboo and wicker furniture in coordinating tropical and animal print fabrics.*

TIP  Remember that there are many everyday things that can be used as drapery rods. Our burlap curtain is hung on a piece of bamboo from the floral department.

Highlight the room with a terrifically tropical table lamp. A self-adhesive lampshade makes customizing a snap! For carefree coastal comfort, trim a sisal rug by hot-gluing strips of tropical print fabric along the edges. Topped with complementary prints and fun fringe, a wicker trunk adds practical storage to this private paradise. And to complete this natural beauty, frame the windows with burlap drapes hung by leather strips and accented with beaded tassels. Even these tailored treatments are made using our quick-and-easy fusing methods.

Fashion your own retreat with an easy-to-transform director's chair and tray table. A framed print comes to life with fabric matting, while a bottle and basket go from ordinary to outstanding with a crown of fabric and beaded trims. Floor and accent pillows add a pampering touch.

**TIP** Explore the many products available to the non-sewer. The neck-roll pillow and the plaid pillow were created using special foam pillow forms, making it quick and easy to create decorative accents for your room.

# TROPICAL LAMPSHADE

*from page 10*

**Supplies**
- self-adhesive lampshade
- two coordinating fabrics
- hot glue gun
- $\frac{7}{8}$"w bias fabric trim (p. 76) to fit around bottom of lampshade
- $\frac{3}{4}$"w fusible web tape
- beaded trim
- gimp trim

**Techniques You'll Need**
- Fusing Basics (p. 72)
- Fabric Trim (p. 76)
- Bonding with Glue (p. 77)

1. Follow manufacturer's instructions to cover lampshade with fabric.
2. Follow Step 1 of Fabric Trim, then glue fabric trim along bottom edge of shade.
3. Glue beaded trim along bottom edge of fabric trim.
4. Wrapping width to inside of shade, glue gimp along top edge of shade.

**TIP** Self-adhesive lampshades come in a variety of shapes and sizes. Use decorator fabric to add a custom no-sew touch to any room in the house! They come complete with their own pattern attached to the shade so you can cut the correct shape in no time!

# SISAL RUG

*from page 10*

**Supplies**
- fabric
- sisal rug (ours is 36"x60")
- $\frac{7}{8}$"w fusible web tape
- hot glue gun

**Techniques You'll Need**
- Fusing Basics (p. 72)
- Single Hem (p. 76)
- Bonding with Glue (p. 77)

1. For borders, cut one 6" wide strip of fabric to fit each edge of your rug.

2. Make a 1" single hem along both long edges of each fabric strip.
3. With width of strip wrapped to back, glue fabric strips along short, then long edges of rug.

# WICKER TRUNK

*from page 10*

**Supplies**
- $\frac{1}{8}$" thick foam core board
- wicker trunk with lid
- batting
- fabric for background
- fabric for side strips
- fusible web
- 1"w fusible web tape
- $1\frac{1}{2}$"w ribbon
- hot glue gun
- 2" fringe trim

**Techniques You'll Need**
- Fusing Basics (p. 72)
- Bonding with Glue (p. 77)

1. Cut foam core to fit trunk lid. Draw around foam core on batting and the wrong side of background fabric. Cut out batting and fabric 1" outside drawn lines.
2. For side strips, cut two 5" wide strips of fabric to fit across background fabric. Fuse side strips onto each side of background fabric.
3. Fuse web tape along center of ribbon; center and fuse ribbon along raw edges where fabrics overlap.
4. Center batting, then foam core, on wrong side of fused fabric piece. Folding fabric like a package, glue excess fabric to back of foam core.
5. Glue fringe around edges of foam core, gently bending at corners. Glue foam core to top of trunk.

# TRAY TABLE

*from page 12*

**Supplies**
- poster board
- tray table
- fabric
- spray adhesive
- craft glue

**Techniques You'll Need**
- Bonding with Glue (p. 77)

1. Cut a piece of poster board to fit inside your tray. Cut a piece of fabric 1" larger on all sides than poster board.
2. Use spray adhesive to cover poster board with fabric, wrapping and gluing excess to back.
3. Place covered poster board in tray.

**TIP** Have a tray but no stand? Make an instant table by placing your tray on top of a luggage rack! Adding a glass top to the tray creates a memory box table!

# BURLAP DRAPES

*from page 11*

### Supplies
- decorative curtain rod with mounting brackets
- burlap
- fusible web
- awl
- 1/8"w leather strips
- beaded tassels

### Techniques You'll Need
- Measuring Your Window (p. 122)
- Fusing Basics (p. 72)

1. Follow manufacturer's instructions to mount brackets and rod at desired position.
2. Measure window from top of rod to floor for curtain length and between brackets for curtain width. Add 4" to length; for each curtain, cut one piece of burlap this size.
3. For each header, cut a 4" wide strip of fusible web. Fuse web along width of burlap 12" from top edge. Press top edge of burlap 16" to front, so web is fused in the fold. Make a 4" fringe along bottom of header.
4. For tie holes, use an awl to carefully poke evenly spaced holes 2" from top of header. For each tie, thread two 32" lengths of leather through one hole; thread a beaded tassel onto leather at front of header. Bring ends of leather lengths to top of header and tie in a knot. Tie another knot 2" from leather ends.
5. Make a 1" fringe along bottom edge of curtain.
6. Thread curtain onto rod and hang.

**HOW TO** To fringe burlap, firmly grasp the first thread along the cut edge of the fabric and pull. Gently pull one row of thread at a time until you reach the desired length.

# BURLAP FLOOR PILLOW

*from page 13*

### Supplies
- two 28" burlap squares
- 3" thick x 24" square of foam
- embroidery floss
- hot glue gun
- two 100" lengths of 3" fringe trim

### Techniques You'll Need
- Bonding with Glue (p. 77)

1. Refer to "How to" tip (above) to make a 1" fringe along edges of burlap squares.
2. Center foam between burlap pieces; pin pieces together. Using six strands of floss, sew a loose running stitch in burlap pieces next to foam.
3. Trimming lengths to fit, glue fringe along running stitches.

# DIRECTOR'S CHAIR

*from page 12*

### Supplies
- director's chair
- two coordinating fabrics
- 7/8"w fusible web tape
- stapler
- fusible web
- hot glue gun
- 1"w gimp trim
- 3 1/2" tassel trim

### Techniques You'll Need
- Single Hem (p. 76)
- Fusing Basics (p. 72)
- Bonding with Glue (p. 77)

1. Measure depth of chair seat; measure length of seat as shown in photo 1. Add 2" to each measurement; cut a piece of fabric this size.
2. Make a 1" single hem along edges of fabric.
3. Pin fabric to chair seat. Staple fabric over canvas along bottom of seat.
4. Measure height of canvas; measure length as shown in photo 2. Add 2" to each measurement; cut a piece of coordinating fabric this size. Slide chair back canvas off chair.
5. Make a 1" single hem along edges of fabric.
6. Fuse web to back of fabric; remove paper backing. Align fabric on chair back canvas; wrapping fabric to back of canvas, fuse in place.
7. Glue gimp trim 1" from top of chair back. Glue tassel trim along bottom edge of chair back. Slide chair back onto chair.

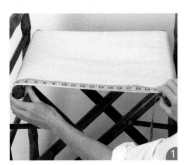

# FRAMED PRINT

*from page 12*

**Supplies**
- matted and framed print
- fabric
- spray adhesive
- fabric glue

**Techniques You'll Need**
- Bonding with Glue (p. 77)

1. Remove matted print from frame; remove print from mat. Cut a piece of fabric 1" larger on all sides than mat. Place mat on wrong side of fabric; draw around inside of mat on fabric. Cut fabric 1" inside drawn line.

2. Use spray adhesive to cover mat with fabric. Clip outside and inside corners; wrap and glue excess fabric to back.
3. Replace print and mat in frame.

# BEADED BOTTLE

*from page 13*

**Supplies**
- 13"h glass bottle with glass stopper
- two coordinating fabrics
- fusible web
- hot glue gun
- 1¼" beaded trim with ribbon flange
- embroidery floss
- two 2" tassels cut from a tassel trim scrap

**Techniques You'll Need**
- Fusing Basics (p. 72)
- Single Hem (p. 76)
- Bonding with Glue (p. 77)

1. Measure around your bottle; add 1". For bottom band, cut one fabric 3½" wide by determined measurement.
2. For top band, add 1" to bottle measurement; cut a strip from remaining fabric 3" wide by determined measurement.

3. Make a 1" single hem on one long edge of each band. Butting raw edges together and overlapping at back, wrap fabrics around bottle and glue in place.
4. Glue trim along raw edges between fabrics.
5. Use floss to tie tassels to bottle stopper.

# DECORATIVE BASKET

*from page 13*

**Supplies**
- round wicker basket with lid
- fabric
- burlap
- ⅞"w fusible web tape
- fusible web
- hot glue gun
- 1"w gimp trim
- beaded tassel

**Techniques You'll Need**
- Single Hem (p. 76)
- Fusing Basics (p. 72)
- Bonding with Glue (p. 77)

1. Measure height of basket to lid; add 1". Measure around basket; add 1". Cut fabric the determined measurements.
2. Measure around basket; add 1". Cut a 2¾" wide strip of burlap the determined measurement. Refer to "How to" tip (p. 15) to make a 1" fringe along one long edge (bottom) of burlap.
3. Make a 1" single hem along bottom edge of fabric. Fuse burlap (use web only on non-fringed area) along

top edge of fabric so that fringe is near the center of background fabric.
4. Glue gimp trim along top edge of burlap.
5. Overlapping at back, wrap fabric around basket and glue in place.
6. Add beaded tassel to lid. You may need to unscrew lid handle, slide tassel on, then reattach handle.

## NECK-ROLL PILLOW

*from page 13*

### Supplies
- June Tailor® Deco-Wrap® No-Sew Neck-roll Pillow
- 5/8 yd fabric to cover pillow
- 1/4 yd coordinating fabric for center strip
- 7/8"w fusible web tape
- hot glue gun
- 5/8 yd of 2" tassel trim

### Techniques You'll Need
- Fusing Basics (p. 72)
- Single Hem (p. 76)
- Bonding with Glue (p. 77)

1. Follow manufacturer's instructions to cover neck roll pillow with fabric.

2. Cut an 8½"x22" piece of coordinating fabric. Make a 1" single hem along one short edge. Wrap fabric around pillow; overlap short edges with hemmed edge on top and glue in place.
3. Beginning at seam on back, glue trim along long edges of center fabric piece.

## FABRIC FLAP PILLOW

*from page 13*

### Supplies
- 7/8"w fusible web tape
- 5"x20" (bottom) and 8"x20" (top) coordinating fabric pieces for flap
- tacky glue
- 20" length of cording with flange
- 20" length of beaded trim with a ribbon flange
- hot glue gun
- 18" Basic Knife-Edge Pillow (p. 88)

### Techniques You'll Need
- Fusing Basics (p. 72)
- Single Hem (p. 76)
- Bonding with Glue (p. 77)

1. For flap, fuse web tape along one long edge on wrong side of bottom flap fabric piece and on right side of top flap fabric piece. Overlapping edges, fuse bottom piece to top piece.

2. Make a 1" single hem along top and side edges of combined 12"x20" fabric piece. Fold bottom fabric of flap in half to wrong side and fuse in place.
3. Use tacky glue to adhere lipped cording along raw edges and to back of flap. Adhere flange of trim along lip of cording.
4. Hot glue top edge of flap to top edge of pillow.

## PLAID PILLOW

*from page 13*

### Supplies
- 1½ yds fabric
- June Tailor® Deco-Wrap® No-Sew Square Pillow
- hot glue gun
- 7" tassel
- 2" dia. fabric-covered button

### Techniques You'll Need
- Bonding with Glue (p. 77)

1. Follow manufacturer's instructions to cut fabric and wrap pillow.
2. Glue hanger of tassel into slit in pillow; glue button to center of pillow.

**TIP** Instead of a button, hot glue a silk flower, a bow, a small framed picture, or a piece of jewelry to the center of your pillow!

# timeless
# TEA ROOM

*With its story-telling patterns woven in rich hues, toile exudes a timeless beauty that fills a room with grace and charm. The ever-popular prints are excellent for dressing windows and furniture. They can also be used to create clever accessories, such as the ones in this divine dining room.*

Toile, which originated in the early-18th century, is still a favorite choice of fabric for interior decorating. The large patterns add visual interest and texture to the room. A single panel drapery is ideal for showcasing the pleasing pastoral scene, while tassel trim adds a fun finishing touch.

TIP Save those scraps of fabric for small accent projects. It only takes a 16" square to make a napkin. Fringe the fabric edges to finish. Mix and match patterns for a fun decorator look!

Your dinette will define beauty when covered with a table topper that frames the toile print with ribbon and a coordinating check fabric. Easy-to-make fringed seat cushions are sure to be conversation pieces.

A basket liner, made from fabric selected to correspond to the toile print, spruces up a plain wicker container. Revamp a serving tray by covering the bottom with coordinating fabric, and then drape it with a harmonizing hand towel. Using a variety of complementary fabrics lends a unifying feel to the room. A refurbished buffet, sporting toile side panels, provides functional finesse.

Create this regal lampshade simply by hot gluing braid along the top edge of the shade and fringed trim along the bottom. It's quick and easy, but oh-so beautiful!

**TIP** Unique lamps, such as this one made from an urn (right), can be fashioned from bottles, vases, teapots ... a lamp adaptor kit from your craft store is all you need for a one-of-a-kind conversation piece.

# SINGLE PANEL DRAPERY

*from page 20*

**Supplies**
- two 1"w conventional rods and mounting brackets
- fabric for panels
- fabric for panel trims
- $7/8$"w fusible web tape
- fusible web
- hot glue gun
- tassel trim
- two drapery tieback mountings with hardware
- two large drapery tiebacks with tassels

**Techniques You'll Need**
- Measuring Your Window (p. 122)
- Fusing Basics (p. 72)
- Joining Fabric Panels (if needed; p. 109)
- Single Hem (p. 76)
- Bonding with Glue (p. 77)

1. For each panel, leaving 2" for header, follow manufacturer's instructions to mount brackets and rod at desired position in window.

2. Measure window from top of rod to floor for panel length and between brackets for panel width; add 1" to width and 24" to length (6" for casing and 18" for a "puddled" hem); cut a piece of fabric this size, joining fabric as needed.

3. Make a 1" single hem along one side edge (outer edge) of panel.

4. Cut a 6" wide strip of trim fabric the same length as panel, piecing as necessary.

5. For fabric trim, matching wrong sides and long raw edges, press trim fabric strip in half. Fuse 3" wide strips of web to wrong side of trim on each side of fold; remove paper backing. Inserting unhemmed edge of panel into fold in trim, fuse trim along edge of panel.

6. Glue a length of tassel trim along raw edge of fabric trim on front of panel.

7. For header and casing, cut two 2" wide strips of fusible web to equal the width of the panel. Press top of panel 6" to wrong side; unfold. Fuse one web strip to wrong side along raw edge and the second strip along fold (photo 1); remove paper backing, refold, and fuse in place.

8. Attach tieback mounting into window trim or wall at desired placement for tieback.

9. Thread curtain onto rod and hang; wrap tieback around curtain and attach to mounting.

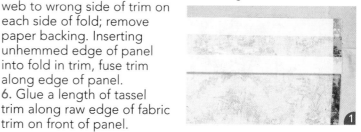

# TABLE TOPPER

*from page 21*

**Supplies**
- $7/8$"w fusible web tape
- 19" square of fabric
- fusible interfacing
- fusible web
- 14" square of toile fabric
- hot glue gun
- $1 2/3$ yds flat trim

**Techniques You'll Need**
- Fusing Basics (p. 72)
- Bonding with Glue (p. 77)

1. Fuse web tape along edges on wrong side of 19" fabric square; remove paper backing.

2. Press one corner of 19" square diagonally to wrong side as shown in photo 1. Repeat for remaining corners. Fuse each edge of fabric piece to wrong side.

3. Fuse interfacing, then fuse web, to wrong side of toile fabric. Cut a 13" square from toile fabric; remove paper backing. Center and fuse toile square to right side of hemmed fabric square.

4. Gently bending around the corners, glue trim along edges of toile square.

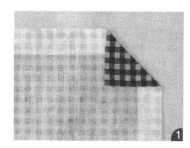

# SEAT CUSHION

*from page 21*

**Supplies**
- electric knife
- 14" dia. foam circle pillow form (makes two cushions)
- two 16" (for bottom) and two 18" (for top) dia. fabric circles
- embroidery floss
- hot glue gun
- $2 1/2$ yds of 1" fringe trim

**Techniques You'll Need**
- Bonding with Glue (p. 77)

1. Use knife to cut pillow form in half lengthwise (rounded side is top).

2. For each cushion, center one form half between wrong sides of fabric circles. Use six strands of embroidery floss to work a loose running stitch in fabric pieces close to edges of form and knot ends; use pinking shears to trim excess fabric to $3/4$".

3. Glue trim along edges of fabric, covering stitching.

**TIP** Hot glue ribbon ends or other trim to underside of cushion to create chairback ties.

## SERVING TRAY

*from page 22*

**Supplies**
- serving tray with a removable or missing bottom
- saw and wood (if needed)
- sandpaper and tack cloth (if needed)
- fabric
- spray adhesive
- hot glue gun

**Techniques You'll Need**
- Bonding with Glue (p. 77)

1. If needed, cut a piece of wood to fit in tray bottom; sand, then wipe wood with tack cloth.
2. Cut a piece of fabric large enough to cover wood piece and wrap to back.
3. Use spray adhesive to attach fabric to wood piece; glue excess fabric to back of wood.
4. Place covered wood piece in tray.

**TIP** If you want to make a changeable or seasonal fabric tray cover to fit a tray bottom, cut a piece of thin cardboard to fit in the tray and cover it with fabric; make one for each season. Fuse on a piece of vinyl to make it spillproof.

## HAND TOWEL

*from page 22*

**Supplies**
- fabric
- hand towel
- fusible web
- fabric glue
- decorative trims

**Techniques You'll Need**
- Fusing Basics (p. 72)
- Bonding with Glue (p. 77)

*If needed, use straight pins to hold fabric trim in place until glue is dry.*

1. Cut a strip of fabric to fit across one end of towel and wrap to back. Fuse a strip of web to wrong side of fabric piece; remove paper backing and fuse in place.

2. Wrapping ends to back, glue trim along top and bottom edges of fabric piece.

## BUFFET

*from page 23*

**Supplies**
- sandpaper
- buffet with the doors removed
- tack cloth
- red and cream paint
- paintbrushes
- walnut and pine water-based wood stains
- soft cloth
- foam core board
- fabric
- heavy-duty spray adhesive

**Techniques You'll Need**
- Bonding with Glue (p. 77)

1. Sand buffet and wipe with tack cloth to remove dust.
2. Paint the top of the buffet red and the remainder of the buffet cream.
3. Apply walnut stain to top of buffet and pine stain to remainder of buffet, then while still wet, wipe away excess stain with soft cloth. To highlight areas, dampen cloth and continue to wipe until desired look is achieved.

4. For each fabric panel, measure the width and height of the buffet side inset; cut a piece of foam core the determined measurements. Centering fabric design as desired, draw around foam core on wrong side of fabric; cut out fabric piece 2" outside drawn lines. Wrapping and gluing ends to back, use spray adhesive to cover foam core with fabric and to adhere fabric panel to side of buffet.

## BASKET LINER

*from page 22*

**Supplies**
- basket
- fabric
- $7/8$"w fusible web
- hot glue gun
- fringe trim
- flat trim

**Techniques You'll Need**
- Fusing Basics (p. 72)
- Single Hem (p. 76)
- Bonding with Glue (p. 77)

1. Measure basket bottom width and add 2"; measure basket length from top back edge, along bottom to top front edge and add desired amount for overhang on both sides of basket, plus 2". Cut a piece of fabric the determined measurements.
2. Make a 1" single hem along edges of fabric piece.

3. Wrapping ends to the back of the liner, glue a length of fringe along one end of liner; repeat to glue a length of flat trim above the fringe. (If desired, repeat for remaining end of liner.)
4. Drape liner in basket.

# fruit punch
## PIZZAZZ

You'll drink in the beauty of this refreshing room every time you enter it! The furniture and accessories are bursting with color in a fun, fruity palette to add punch to the crisp white walls. Sure to liven your spirits, every day will feel like a party.

These vibrantly hued accents are like candy for the eyes! Orange and pink polka dots provide a playful contrast to both the green and white swirls and the black and white stripes. You'll have the perfect spot to relax after you cover your chair seat with a fresh, funky print. An accent table goes from so-so to so-fun when embellished with rickrack-bordered fabric on top and a coordinating print on the drawer facing. A pillow cover and a striped pillow show the diversity of this seating staple. And accented with black beaded trim, the flirty lampshade is pretty in pink and white.

TIP When coordinating fabrics, make a swatch book to take with you on your shopping adventures. It will make matching fabric, trims, and paint choices so much easier!

29

Create this lighthearted, beribboned chandelier in a flash by covering the shades in a green and white swirl fabric set off with black trim and pink ball fringe. A plant stand filled with flowers will brighten the room, especially when the plants are placed in festively painted pots. Use a shade kit to fashion quick-and-easy window treatments to coordinate with your room. For eye-catching artwork that can be hung in a window or on the wall, fuse your choice of fabric onto an artist canvas and appliqué a flower in the center.

TIP  Use suction cup hangers on the windows to display the appliquéd floral prints – you don't have to mar the window trim and they're easily concealed by the shade.

## STRIPED PILLOW

*from page 29*

### Supplies
- four 19" squares of fusible web
- two 19" squares of striped fabric
- two 19" squares of muslin
- 3/8"w fusible web tape
- 1/2"w velvet ribbon
- polyester batting
- 2 1/2" dia. fabric-covered shank button

### Techniques You'll Need
- Fusing Basics (p. 72)
- Basic Knife-Edge Pillow (p. 88)

1. Fuse web squares on the wrong side of both fabric squares; do not remove paper backing. Cut each striped square along the diagonals to make four equal triangles (eight total); remove paper backing.
2. Using triangles with matching stripe direction from each set, arrange four triangle pieces on each muslin square. Fuse in place; trim to 18".

3. Fuse web tape along center on wrong side of ribbon. Wrapping ends to back, fuse ribbon in an "X" over raw edges of triangles on each square.
4. Use pillow front and back to make a Basic Knife-Edge Pillow.
5. Pulling thread tightly to "tuft" pillow, sew button to center of pillow.

## PILLOW COVER

*from page 29*

### Supplies
- rectangular pillow form
- fabric for main pillow cover section
- ffabric for cuff
- fusible web
- fusible web tape
- hot glue gun
- ball fringe
- velvet ribbon to match ball fringe
- velvet ribbon to contrast with ball fringe

### Techniques You'll Need
- Fusing Basics (p. 72)
- Single Hem (p. 76)

1. Measure width and length of your pillow form.
2. Add 2" to pillow width and double pillow length; cut one piece of fabric this size for main section.
3. Add 2" to pillow width; cut two pieces of cuff fabric 7" by the determined width measurement.
4. Fuse web tape along one long edge on wrong side of each cuff. Piece web tape along each short edge on right side of main section. Overlapping fused edges, fuse one cuff to each end of pillowcase. Make 1" single hems along remaining long edge of each cuff.

5. Wrapping ends to back, glue ball fringe over raw fabric edge between main section and cuff. Glue matching ribbon onto flange of ball fringe; glue contrasting ribbon next to flange of ball fringe.
6. Fuse web tape on right side along each long edge of pillow cover; do not remove paper backing. Matching right sides and cuff ends, press pillowcase in half. Remove paper backing and fuse long edges together.
7. Turn pillowcase right side out and insert pillow form.

## ACCENT TABLE

*from page 28*

### Supplies
- sandpaper and tack cloth
- accent table with drawer
- primer
- paint and paintbrush
- poster board
- two coordinating fabrics
- craft glue
- jumbo rickrack
- fusible web
- pressing cloth

### Techniques You'll Need
- Bonding with Glue (p. 77)
- Fusing Basics (p. 72)

1. Sand table as necessary and wipe with tack cloth to remove dust.
2. Prime, then paint table.
3. Measure the width and length of the top of the table. Subtract 2" from length and 1" from width; cut a piece of poster board this size.
4. Draw around poster board on wrong side of one fabric. Cut out fabric 2" outside drawn lines. Wrap edges of fabric to back of poster board and glue in place.

5. With one long edge of poster board even with back of table, use glue poster board to table. Center and glue rickrack, covering edges of poster board.
6. Remove drawer and knob(s); measure drawer front. Fuse a piece of web to a piece of coordinating fabric that fits drawer front; use pressing cloth to fuse fabric to drawer. Reattach knobs (through fabric) and reinsert drawer in table.

**Supplies**
- self-adhesive lampshade
- fabric
- tacky glue
- gimp trim
- clothespins
- beaded trim with flange
- black ribbon trim

**Techniques You'll Need**
- Fusing Basics (p. 72)
- Bonding with Glue (p. 77)

Use clothespins to secure trims on lampshade until glue is dry.

1. Follow manufacturer's instructions to cover lampshade with fabric.
2. Glue gimp trim along top of lampshade.
3. Glue beaded trim along bottom of lampshade.
4. Glue black ribbon trim on top of beaded trim flange.

**Supplies**
- chairs with padded seats
- fabric
- polyester batting
- staple gun

1. Remove seat from chair. Draw around seat on wrong side of fabric. Cut out fabric 3" outside drawn line. Cut batting same size as seat (you may need to cut several layers of batting for desired thickness of seat). Layer batting, then seat on wrong side of fabric (photo 1).
2. Pulling fabric taut, staple the center of opposite fabric edges to bottom of seat (photo 2).
3. Working from the center to the corners, stretching the fabric evenly, and rotating the seat after each staple, repeat with the other two edges (photo 3).

4. Staple the fabric at the center of each corner, then ease and staple the fabric through the rest of the corner (photo 4).
5. Reattach seat in chair.

**TIP** An electric staple gun is a good investment. You will be surprised at the home projects that can be done with this tool!

### Supplies
- 14"x18" artist canvas panel
- fusible web
- 18" square background fabric
- fabric with large flowers
- hot glue gun
- 1/2"w velvet ribbon
- 3/4"w satin ribbon
- suction hanger

### Techniques You'll Need
- Fusing Basics (p. 72)
- Bonding with Glue (p. 77)

*We recommend using a repositionable single or double sided paper-backed sticky fusible web for making appliqués. You can finger press the appliqué in place because of the sticky adhesive under the paper backing. This allows it to be repositioned until ready to heat set it with the iron.*

*If using a basic paper-backed fusible web, the appliqué can be temporarily held in place by lightly touching it with the tip of the iron. If your appliqué is not in the desired position, carefully lift and reposition before fusing in place.*

1. For each appliquéd picture, cut artist canvas to 14" square. Wrapping and fusing excess to back, fuse background fabric to canvas.
2. Fuse a piece of web to the wrong side of the large flower fabric over the flower you wish to use as your appliqué (photo 1). Do not remove the paper backing.
3. Cut out the appliqué along the edges of the flower (photo 2); remove the paper backing.
4. Center your appliqué, web side down, on the canvas; fuse your appliqué in place (photo 3).
5. Wrapping and gluing ends to back, glue ribbon along each edge of the canvas.
6. Cut a length of satin ribbon; glue one end to the top back of the canvas. Tie remaining end onto suction hanger; attach suction hanger to window.

### Supplies
- spray primer
- flowerpots
- white semigloss spray paint
- masking tape
- acrylic paints and paintbrushes
- hot glue gun
- ribbon
- trim

### Techniques You'll Need
- Bonding with Glue (p. 77)

1. Prime flowerpots. Spray paint pots white. Mask rim of pot and paint base desired color.
2. Glue ribbon and trim around rim of pots.

**TIP** Flowerpots can hold more than just plants. Decorate them to match your bath decor and fill with rolled up hand towels and decorative soaps. Use them on your desk to hold pens, pencils, rulers, and scissors. And they are perfect as a candleholder for a large pillar candle.

## CHANDELIER

*from page 30*

**Supplies**
- chandelier with small lampshades
- spray paint
- tissue paper
- fabric
- spray adhesive
- craft glue
- gimp trim
- clothespins
- ball fringe
- ribbon trim
- ribbon

**Techniques You'll Need**
- Bonding with Glue (p. 77)

Use clothespins to secure trims on lampshades until glue is dry.

1. Remove shades; spray paint chandelier.
2. Make a tissue paper pattern for lampshades by wrapping paper around one shade (tape in place), tracing the top and bottom edges, and marking a vertical line for the seam. Remove paper from shade and cut out pattern.
3. For each lampshade, pin the pattern to your fabric, then cut the fabric 1" outside the pattern edges on all sides. Centering fabric on shade, use spray adhesive to adhere fabric to shade; trim the fabric even with the top and bottom edges of the shade.

4. Glue gimp trim along top edge of each shade.
5. Glue ball fringe along bottom edge of each shade; glue ribbon trim to flange of ball fringe.
6. Tie a length of ribbon into a bow around stem of chandelier beneath each lampshade.

**Alternative:** If your chandelier did not come with lampshades, buy the self-adhesive kind to fit your bulbs. Follow the manufacturer's instructions to cover the shades with fabric, then refer to the instructions here to finish decorating your shades.

## WINDOW SHADE

*from page 31*

**Supplies**
- tension rod
- two coordinating fabrics
- $7/8$" wide fusible web tape
- hot glue gun
- jumbo rickrack

**Techniques You'll Need**
- Measuring Your Window (p. 122)
- Fusing Basics (p. 72)
- Single Hem (p. 76)
- Bonding with Glue (p. 77)

1. Measure desired width and height of shade in window. Add 2" to width and subtract 4" from height; cut fabric to determined measurements.

2. For rod pocket, fuse a length of tape along top edge of fabric; do not remove paper backing. Press top edge 3" to wrong side. Unfold, remove paper backing, and press again to fuse in place.
3. Fuse a length of web tape along the bottom edge of the fabric on the wrong side.
4. Cut an 8" strip of coordinating fabric the same width as determined in Step 1. Fuse a length of web tape along one width edge on the right side.
5. Overlapping taped edges, fuse coordinating fabric along bottom of shade fabric.
6. Make a 1" single hem along each side of shade.

7. Wrapping ends to back, glue rickrack along seam between fabrics.
8. Thread shade on rod and hang in window.

**TIP** For quick roller shades, use June Tailor® shade kits to make dressings to fit your windows.

# modern
# RETREAT

A striking combination of silver and brown permeates this room with the cool feeling of shiny silk and steel tempered by the warm feeling of wood and brushed suede. Used definitively in modern design, the clean lines and minimal accessories emphasize the creative color contrast. The result is a restful, rejuvenating retreat.

**TIP** We made a headboard for our bed using plywood, but you can also create the illusion of one by simply gluing these suede squares to the wall behind your bed.

The focal point of this room is definitely the sleek bed. Upholstered in mocha microsuede, the stately headboard is dreamy! Simple squares lend to the linear look of the room, while buttons covered in the same material add architectural detail. Strips of suede are used to trim a lampshade and give it sophisticated appeal. Square pillows mimic the design of the headboard but are tufted to provide an extra measure of comfort. A luxurious throw, made from coordinating fabric embellished with tassel fringe, drapes the bed in touchable texture.

# HEADBOARD

*from page 38*

### Supplies
- 55"x52" piece of plywood (to fit double bed)
- foam core board
- 1" thick foam sheets
- microsuede
- fifteen 2" dia. buttons from covered button kits
- embroidery floss
- hot glue gun
- heavy-duty screws

### Techniques You'll Need
- Bonding with Glue (p. 77)

1. Cut fifteen 11" squares each from foam core and foam sheets. Use spray adhesive to adhere one foam sheet square to one foam core square. Draw an "X" on the back of each foam core square from corner to corner.

2. Cut fifteen 15" microsuede squares.
3. For each square, center a foam core piece, "X" side up, on wrong side of one suede square. Wrap and glue edges of microsuede to back of foam core.
4. Follow manufacturer's instructions to cover buttons with microsuede. Using the center of the "X" for placement and sewing through all layers, sew a button to the center front of each microsuede square.
5. Starting at the top, place microsuede squares on plywood, arranging in three rows of five squares each. Hot glue squares in place on headboard.
6. Use heavy-duty screws to attach plywood to the head of your bed.

**TIP** You can create a headboard in any size — one square at a time. Make them larger or smaller, use more of them or less of them to make the perfect headboard size.

# ELONGATED PILLOW

*from page 38*

### Supplies
- 27"x32" piece of fabric
- 7/8"w fusible web tape
- two 8"x11½" strips of microsuede
- pressing cloth
- fusible web
- polyester fiberfill

### Techniques You'll Need
- Fusing Basics (p. 72)

*Always use a pressing cloth when pressing microsuede.*

1. Fuse web tape along each long edge on right side of fabric; remove paper backing. Matching right sides, fuse long edges together to form a tube. Turn right side out.

2. Matching wrong sides, press each microsuede strip in half lengthwise. Unfold and fuse pieces of web to back of each strip. Wrap one strip around one end of pillow so that pressed fold covers raw edges of fabric; fuse in place.
3. Stuff pillow with fiberfill. Wrap remaining strip around other end of pillow; fuse in place.

# UNISHAM

*from page 38*

### Supplies
- pressing cloth
- two 8"x44" strips of microsuede
- fusible web
- 44"x62" piece of fabric
- 7/8"w fusible web tape

### Techniques You'll Need
- Fusing Basics (p. 72)

*Always use a pressing cloth when pressing microsuede.*

1. Fuse a length of fusible web to wrong side of microsuede strips; do not remove paper backing. Press strips in half lengthwise; unfold and remove paper backing. Insert each end of fabric into fold of one strip and fuse in place.

2. Fuse web tape to right side of one long edge and to wrong side of remaining long edge of combined fabrics; remove paper backing.
3. Overlap long edges with web tape between fabric edges and fuse in place to form unisham.

## TUFTED SQUARE PILLOWS

*from page 39*

### Supplies
- two 17" squares of silk fabric
- $7/8$"w fusible web tape
- 1" thick foam sheet
- embroidery floss

### Techniques You'll Need
- Fusing Basics (p. 72)
- Basic Knife-Edge Pillow (p. 88)

1. Following Steps 1–4 and leaving one entire side open for stuffing, use fabric squares to make a Basic Knife-Edge Pillow.
2. Cut two 15" squares of foam. Pushing all the seam allowances to back of pillow, insert foam sheets in pillow. Fuse seam closed.

3. To tuft pillow, find center of pillow. Using twelve strands of embroidery floss, sew through all layers of pillow; knot at back. From center, measure out $4\frac{1}{2}$", stitch, and knot again. Repeat to tuft pillow a total of nine times in a square pattern.

## SIMPLE SHADE

*from page 39*

### Supplies
- lampshade
- microsuede fabric
- spray adhesive

### Techniques You'll Need
- Bonding with Glue (p. 77)

1. Measure around the top and bottom edges of your lampshade; add 1" to each measurement. Cut one $3/4$" wide strip of fabric each determined length.
2. Use spray adhesive to adhere fabric strips around top and bottom of lampshade.

**TIP** Sometimes you don't have to do much to give a custom look to a purchased item. Two simple stripes of fabric were all this lamp needed!

## LUXURIOUS THROW

*from page 39*

### Supplies
- $1\frac{1}{4}$ yds of 54"w heavy-weight fabric
- $7/8$"w fusible web tape
- fabric glue
- $5\frac{1}{2}$ yds tassel trim

### Techniques You'll Need
- Fusing Basics (p. 72)
- Single Hem (p. 76)

1. Make a 1" single hem along long edges of fabric.
2. Wrapping ends to back, glue fringe along short edges to complete throw.

**TIP** This throw would also look wonderful draped over a wooden table as a table topper.

# **moroccan** OASIS

Transform your bedroom into a Moroccan oasis by choosing fabrics in an exotic mix of rich jewel tones — garnet, sapphire, and emerald sparked with gold — that reflect the mystique of a land far away. In addition to color, the main ingredients needed to add Moroccan flavor to your room are layers of texture and intricate patterns with beaded detail.

Create a stunning backdrop for an intimate seating area by hanging a pair of rich garnet-colored draperies on a decorative rod. The lush curtains will instantly add a sense of warmth and coziness to your space. For a hint of dramatic flair, line the inside vertical hems with beaded trim. Dress up your bed with a colorful, beribboned duvet and layers of pillows that beckon you to lie back and relax. Gold ribbon emblazons the solid-colored shams, while ornate, multi-colored patterns highlight the pillows. The eye-catching array of shapes, sizes, and patterns lends a feeling of an exotic retreat.

**TIP** Bedsheets have ample yardage and sufficient width to avoid piecing large projects — they're also cost-saving! The duvet is backed with a queen-size flat sheet. If you wanted to line the draperies, you could make panels from sheets to clip behind the decorative fabric.

**TIP** The metallic fabric for the basket top was also used on the duvet. It provided inspiration for all the fabrics and trims used in the room. Find your favorite fabric to inspire you!

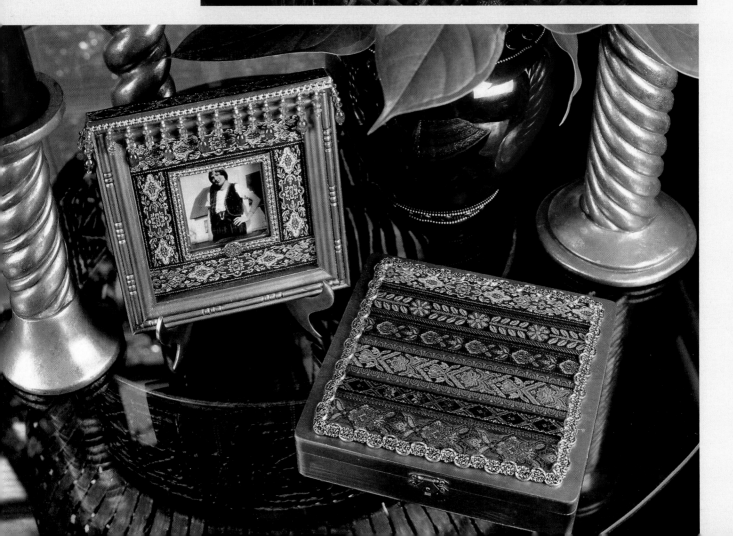

Decorative accents will help you achieve a truly Moroccan style. Mimic the look of authentic, ornately carved wood candlesticks simply by adding a little paint and assorted trims. Woven baskets are a mainstay in Moroccan design. Use vibrant fabric to convert a large lidded basket into a pretty, practical nightstand. Fuse an assortment of woven metallic trims to the lid of a wooden box to create the look of tapestry. You can also use flat trims to fashion a one-of-a-kind photo frame. Top it off with beaded trim for a picture-perfect result.

**Supplies**
• decorative curtain rod with finials and brackets
• fabric
• fusible web
• 1 1/2"w fusible web tape
• hot glue gun
• beaded trim
• clip-on curtain rings

**Techniques You'll Need**
• Measuring Your Window (p. 122)
• Fusing Basics (p. 72)
• Single Hem (p. 76)
• Bonding with Glue (p. 77)

1. Follow manufacturer's instructions to mount brackets and rod at desired position.
2. Measure windows from top of rod to floor for curtain length and between brackets for curtain width. Add 26" to length and 4" to width; for each curtain cut one piece of fabric this size.
3. To make header, cut two 4" wide strips of fusible web. Make a 4" single hem at the top of the curtain using the web. Fold again to make another 4" single hem.

4. Make a 2" single hem on each side of the curtain. Glue beaded trim along one side hem.
5. Evenly space curtain rings along top of curtain. Thread rings onto rod and hang. Tuck bottom edge of curtain under at the floor and arrange fabric for a "puddled" effect.

**Supplies**
• duvet
• two 54" wide coordinating fabrics
• pressing cloth
• 7/8"w fusible web tape
• fusible web
• two flat trims
• flat sheet cut 1" larger than duvet on all sides
• gimp trim
• decorative buttons

**Techniques You'll Need**
• Fusing Basics (p. 72)
• Joining Fabric Panels (p. 109)

1. For center panel, measure length and width of duvet. Add 2" to length; divide width by two and add 2".

Cut one fabric piece these dimensions.
2. For side panels, divide width of duvet by four and add 2". Cut two pieces of remaining fabric these dimensions.
3. Join one side panel to each long edge of center panel.
4. Fuse web tape along back of flat trims. Center and fuse one flat trim along each fused seam.
5. Fuse remaining flat trim along top edge of fused panels.
6. Fuse web tape along side and bottom edges of joined fabrics. Fuse web tape along side and bottom edges of sheet. With right sides

together and leaving top edge open, fuse side and bottom edges of joined fabrics to sheet. Clip corners and turn right side out.
7. Measure the top edge of your duvet cover to determine how many ties you want; our six ties are spaced 12" apart. For each tie, cut two 12" lengths of gimp trim. Press ends of each trim piece 1/2" to wrong side and tack in place. For each tie, sew a button to one end of gimp, then to top edge of duvet cover, matching placement on front and back of cover.
8. Insert duvet and tie cover to secure.

# SHAMS

from page 45

**Supplies**
- fabric
- standard bed pillow
- fusible web
- 3³/₄"w wire-edged ribbon with wire removed
- ⁷/₈"w fusible web tape

**Techniques You'll Need**
- Fusing Basics (p. 72)
- Single Hem (p. 76)

1. Measure width and length of pillow; add 2" to each measurement. Cut a piece of fabric this size. Fuse a length of ribbon 4" from each short edge of fabric.
2. Add 6" to pillow length and 2" to pillow width. Cut a piece of fabric this size; Matching ends cut piece in half. Make a 1" single hem along one short edge of each piece.
3. Overlap hemmed edges at center and pin together for pillow back.

4. Working on right sides and being careful not to overlap tape, fuse web tape along all edges of pillow front and back. Remove paper backing. Place pillow front and back right sides together and fuse edges in place. Remove pins; turn pillow right side out through hemmed edges on pillow back.
5. Insert pillow in sham.

# ROUND PILLOW

from page 45

**Supplies**
- June Tailor® Deco-Wrap® No-Sew Round Pillow
- fabric
- rubber band
- hot glue gun
- brush fringe

**Techniques You'll Need**
- Bonding with Glue (p. 77)

1. Follow pillow manufacturer's instructions to cut fabric. Place pillow on wrong side of fabric with slit in pillow on top. Wrap and gather fabric to front of pillow; secure gathers with rubber band at center. Tuck ends of fabric to the inside of the rubber band and tuck into the slit in pillow.
2. Glue brush fringe around rubber band.

**TIP** This same technique will work on a square pillow, also. And, did you know the pillow is reversible? The opposite side is a smooth round pillow if you want a sleek look!

# RECTANGLE PILLOW

from page 45

**Supplies**
- two coordinating fabrics
- fusible web
- 14" lengths of two flat trims
- ⁷/₈"w fusible web tape
- polyester batting
- hot glue gun
- 14" length of beaded trim

**Techniques You'll Need**
- Fusing Basics (p. 72)
- Basic Knife-Edge Pillow (p. 88)
- Bonding with Glue (p. 77)

1. Cut two 14"x20" pieces from one fabric for front and back of pillow. Cut a 6"x14" piece of coordinating fabric; fuse along one short edge of pillow front.

2. Covering raw edge, fuse one trim along raw edge of fabric on pilloiw front; fuse remaining trim parallel to first trim.
3. Make a Basic Knife-Edge Pillow from pillow front and back.
4. Glue beaded trim next to flat trims.

## SQUARE PILLOW

*from page 45*

**Supplies**
- fabric
- hot glue gun
- trims
- craft fusible interfacing
- 14" Basic Knife-Edge Pillow (p. 88) of coordinating fabric

**Techniques You'll Need**
- Bonding with Glue (p. 77)
- Fusing Basics (p. 72)

1. Cut an 11" square of fabric. Wrapping ends to back, glue trims along each edge of fabric square.
2. Fuse interfacing to back of fabric. Glue fabric square to front of knife-edge pillow.

**TIP** For an exotic look, add beaded tassels to each corner of the pillow. Or, make this pillow *really* large for floor pillow seating.

## PICTURE FRAME

*from page 47*

**Supplies**
- small wooden picture frame
- gold spray paint
- water-based walnut stain
- foam brush
- soft cloth
- hot glue gun
- flat trim
- beaded trim
- exotic button

**Techniques You'll Need**
- Bonding with Glue (p. 77)

1. Spray paint frame gold. Apply stain and wipe off with a soft cloth while it's still wet.
2. Hot glue trim along flat areas of frame; glue beaded trim along top edge of frame. Glue button to bottom edge of frame.

**TIP** This frame can also be glued to the front of a purchased photo album for a special room accent.

## CANDLESTICKS

*from page 47*

**Supplies**
- candlesticks
- acrylic paint and paintbrush
- hot glue
- assorted trims
- candles

**Techniques You'll Need**
- Bonding with Glue (p. 77)

To make these candlesticks, simply paint a few sections of the candlesticks with coordinating colors and hot glue lengths of trims around other sections. Finish with an elegant candle.

**TIP** Glue small glass or wooden plates to the top of these candleholders to save your carpet or flooring from wax drips.

**Supplies**
- poster board
- basket with attached lid
- fabric
- spray adhesive
- hot glue gun
- assorted flat and beaded trims
- beaded tassel

**Techniques You'll Need**
- Bonding with Glue (p. 77)

1. Cut a piece of poster board to fit on top of the basket lid. Draw around poster board on wrong side of fabric. Cut out fabric 1" outside drawn lines.
2. Apply spray adhesive to fabric; cover poster board with fabric, wrapping excess to back.
3. Glue covered poster board to basket lid.
4. Glue trims around lid and base of basket.

5. Cut a 7" length of one wide trim; thread through loop of tassel. Glue ends of trim inside basket so that tassel hangs on outside front of basket.

**TIP** If you can't find beaded trim in the colors you want, simply layer two trims together.

**Supplies**
- gold spray paint
- wooden box with hinged lid
- water-based walnut stain
- foam brush
- soft cloth
- fabric
- pressing cloth
- fusible web tape
- assorted flat trims
- hot glue gun

**Techniques You'll Need**
- Fusing Basics (p. 72)
- Bonding with Glue (p. 77)

1. Spray paint box. Apply stain; while still wet, wipe off excess stain with cloth.
2. Cut a piece of fabric the same size as the top of the box. Use pressing cloth and fuse several trims side by side across fabric. Trim fabric ³/₄" from each edge.
3. Glue fabric to top of box. Glue trim along edges of fused piece.

**TIP** Add a purse handle to top edge of box for an exotic handbag! All your friends will want one, too.

# casual
# COTTAGE

*If you're looking for a relaxing place to while away your weekends, then create a comfy cottage room! The light and airy feel of the cottage style exudes a sense of casual charm that is ideal for year-round decorating.*

**TIP** Cut a piece of fabric to fit each drawer bottom. Coat back of fabric with spray adhesive and press in place.

Revive a wardrobe cabinet with a fresh coat of paint and pretty fabric. Pad one door inset with batting, cover it with fabric, and add ribbons to hold special photos and mementos. Another door, covered with fabric and ribbon, makes an appealing backdrop for a collectible plate. You can wrap up a fuss-free accent in no time using a no-sew pillow form and your choice of embellishments! Embellish a wooden framed mirror in complementary fabric and border it with ribbon and lace to reflect your cottage style. Create unity in your room by repeating some of your fabrics on smaller projects and accent pieces. We made this lovely lampshade with part of the fabric used on the wardrobe. And scraps from the wingback chair and ottoman turn this chest into a real charmer.

You'll love how easy it is to make a plain floor lamp simply delightful. Just cover the shade in a fabric to coordinate with your room and add fanciful fringe. A crisp check is paired with plaid and tasseled trim to create this designer-look ottoman. For a soft, feminine touch, let your table skirt flow into soft "puddles" at the bottom. And keep your eyes open at flea markets for unique finds like the metal tray tabletop we found to top off our table skirt. And can you believe we covered this wingback chair without ever sewing a stitch? Staples and glue do the trick.

**TIP** The nice thing about a "puddled" hem, whether it is on a table skirt or a drapery, is that you really don't have to hem it at all. Poofing the bottom under hides the raw edges of your fabric. If it is a fabric that ravels or frays easily, you may want to cut the raw edge with pinking shears.

## CHEST

*from page 55*

**Supplies**
• small chest
• paint and paintbrush
• heavy-duty fusible web
• two coordinating fabrics
• pressing cloth

**Techniques You'll Need**
• Fusing Basics (p. 72)

1. Remove knobs from chest. Paint as desired.
2. Fuse web to wrong side of both fabrics. Cut one fabric to fit drawer fronts and one to fit top of chest. Use pressing cloth to fuse fabrics to chest, being careful not to touch iron to painted surfaces.
3. Replace knobs.

**TIP** Instead of fusing fabric pieces to your chest, follow découpage glue manufacturer's instructions to adhere the fabric in place. A top coat of the glue seals and protects the fabric.

## LAMPSHADE

*from page 53*

**Supplies**
• self-adhesive lampshade
• fabric
• craft glue
• lace trim
• clothespins
• gimp trim
• hot glue gun
• silk roses

**Techniques You'll Need**
• Bonding with Glue (p. 77)

*Use clothespins to secure trims on lampshade until glue is dry.*

1. Follow manufacturer's instructions to cover lampshade with fabric.

2. Wrapping part of width to inside, glue lace trim around bottom edge of shade.
3. Glue gimp along top edge of shade. Hot glue roses around top edge of shade.

## FABRIC FRAME

*from page 55*

**Supplies**
• mirror with a flat wooden frame
• spray paint
• fabric
• spray adhesive
• lace trim
• narrow satin ribbon

**Techniques You'll Need**
• Bonding with Glue (p. 77)

1. Remove mirror from frame. Spray paint frame.
2. Cut fabric strips to fit along sides of frame, mitering corners. Use spray adhesive to secure fabric to sides of frame.
3. Cut lengths of lace to fit along outside edges of frame, mitering corners. Use spray adhesive to adhere lace to frame.
4. Cut lengths of ribbon to fit along inside edges of frame, overlapping ends. Use spray adhesive to adhere ribbon to frame.
5. Replace mirror in frame.

**TIP** You don't have to be perfect in your cutting – just close. The lace and ribbon trim covers up any small miscut that might be happen. Big mistake? Use wider lace and ribbon.

**Supplies**
- wardrobe cabinet
- paint and paintbrush
- batting
- fabric
- hot glue gun
- narrow ribbon
- ribbon roses
- plate with decorative cutout edges
- two coordinating wide ribbons
- felt

**Techniques You'll Need**
- Bonding with Glue (p. 77)
- Fusing Basics (p. 72)

1. Remove door facings from wardrobe cabinet. Paint wardrobe cabinet as desired.
2. For memo board, draw around door facing on batting and the wrong side of fabric. Cut out batting and fabric 2" outside drawn lines. Center batting, then door facing, on the wrong side of the fabric piece. Pulling the fabric taut, wrap and glue edges of fabric to the back of the door facing.
3. Gluing the ends to the back of the door facing, use lengths of narrow ribbon to make evenly spaced diamonds. Hot glue ribbon roses at each ribbon intersection. Reattach door facing in door.

4. For door with hanging plate, draw around door facing on wrong side of fabric; cut out 2" outside drawn lines. Center door on wrong side of the fabric piece. Pulling the fabric taut, wrap and glue edges of fabric to the back of the door. Glue a length of narrow ribbon along each side of covered door facing.
5. Hang plate from a length of wide ribbon. Glue ribbon ends onto back of covered door facing. Reinsert door facing in door; hot glue a coordinating wide ribbon bow to top of door.
6. Cut a piece of felt slightly smaller than each door facing. Glue to back of door facings to cover raw edges of fabric and ribbon.

# RECTANGLE PILLOW

**Supplies**
- fabric
- June Tailor® Deco-Wrap® No-Sew Rectangle Pillow
- 1¹/₂"w wire-edged ribbon
- hot glue gun
- artificial rose

**Techniques You'll Need**
- Bonding with Glue (p. 77)

1. Follow manufacturer's instructions to cut fabric and wrap pillow.
2. Make a four-loop bow from ribbon; glue to front of pillow. Glue rose to center of bow.

**TIP** Make sure to use wire-edged ribbon for the bow. That way if someone sits or rests on the pillow, the ribbon can later be re-fluffed and shaped again.

## FLOOR LAMP

*from page 56*

**Supplies**
- floor lamp with lampshade
- spray paint
- tissue paper
- fabric
- spray adhesive
- hot glue gun
- narrow gimp trim
- ball fringe
- wide gimp trim (in same width as flange of ball fringe)

**Techniques You'll Need**
- Bonding with Glue (p. 77)

1. Remove shade; spray paint base of lamp.
2. Make a tissue paper pattern for your lampshade by wrapping paper around the shade, tracing the top and bottom edges, and marking a vertical line for the seam. Remove paper and cut out.
3. Pin the pattern to your fabric, then cut the fabric 1" outside the pattern edges on all sides.
4. Use spray adhesive to adhere fabric to shade; trim the fabric even with the top and bottom edges of the shade.
5. Glue narrow gimp trim around top edge of shade.
6. Glue ball fringe around bottom edge of shade; glue wide gimp trim to flange of ball fringe.

## BLUE PLAID OTTOMAN

*from page 56*

**Supplies**
- paint and paintbrush (optional)
- ottoman
- two coordinating fabrics
- staple gun
- ⁷⁄₈"w fusible web tape
- hot glue gun
- cording with flange
- tassel trim

**Techniques You'll Need**
- Fusing Basics (p. 72)
- Single Hem (p. 76)
- Bonding with Glue (p. 77)

1. Paint feet of ottoman if desired.
2. Wrap ottoman in fabric, folding at corners (photo 1); staple along bottom of ottoman. Trim excess fabric.
3. For strip, measure from bottom of cushion to bottom of ottoman; add 1". Cut fabric this width and long enough to wrap around bottom of ottoman and overlap itself by 2".
4. Make a 1" single hem along top edge of fabric strip and along one end. Glue flange of cording along wrong side of top edge. With cording along top edge and overlapping fabric with hemmed end on top, glue fabric around bottom of ottoman.
5. Glue tassel trim along bottom of fabric strip.

## TABLE SKIRT

*from page 56*

**Supplies**
- fabric
- ⁷⁄₈"w fusible web tape

**Techniques You'll Need**
- Fusing Basics (p. 72)
- Measuring Your Table (p. 108)
- Joining Panel Widths (p. 109)
- Cutting a Circle (p. 109)

*We added a purchased metal tray tabletopper on top of our table for a decorative effect.*

1. Measure table; add 18" for a "puddled" hem.
2. To determine the number of fabric widths you need, divide table measurement by the width of your fabric. Round the result up to a whole number; cut this number of fabric widths.
3. Join panel widths, then cut a circle from fabric the measurement determined in Step 1.
4. Place the skirt on the table; tuck edge of fabric under at the floor and arrange folds for a puddled effect.

### Supplies
- paint and paintbrush (optional)
- wingback chair
- fabric
- staple gun
- butter knife
- hot glue gun
- flat trim

### Techniques You'll Need
- Bonding with Glue (p. 77)

1. Paint legs of chair if desired.
2. Remove seat cushion. Refer to photo 1 to drape fabric over the top of the chair back. Centering fabric design as desired, cut fabric to fit chair.
3. Staple fabric in place along top back of chair; trim excess. Leaving 2" excess, trim sides and bottom of fabric. Refer to photo 2 and use back of butter knife to gently push edges of fabric into the gap between cushions. Lightly stuff fabric into the gap at the back of the seat.
4. Drape fabric from the back of the seat to the front of the seat; cut fabric to fit. Staple the fabric at the bottom of seat; trim excess. Lightly stuff fabric into the gap at the back of the seat.
5. Drape fabric around wings. Staple at back; trim and stuff excess into sides at front (photo 3).
6. Carefully remove upholstered front arm covers. For each arm, drape fabric around arm. Staple at bottom and back (photo 4); trim and stuff excess into sides of chair. Refer to photo 5 to gather fabric at front of arm; trim excess and staple in place.
7. Wrap front arm covers with fabric, gluing at back (photo 6). Glue arm covers in place on chair.
8. Drape fabric on back of chair; staple in place and trim excess (photo 7). Glue flat trim over raw edges.
9. Refer to photo 8 to wrap fabric around seat cushion, folding at corners and gluing in place on back. Trim excess fabric as needed. Replace seat cushion in chair.

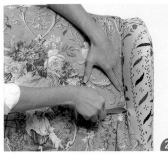

# parisian
# MÉLANGE

Flea markets are treasure troves of unique home decorating items! If you're a flea market fan, you're sure to have obtained a cache of vintage collectibles. Now's the time to get them out, touch them up, and create that wonderful, one-of-a-kind look of which you've always dreamed! Do just a few projects or enough to fill a whole room — the choice is yours and the possibilities are endless!

TIP Adding a border of trim at the top edge of the seat cushion gives it a crisp linear edge much like you would have if the cushion was actually sewn.

Add comfort and character to your room by padding a bench with an inviting seat cushion and plush pillow. This wall hanging — easily created from a piece of scenic tapestry fabric — looks like a prized masterpiece. Revamped with harlequin print fabric and playful tassels, this stool is a real show stopper. Transform a magazine rack from common to classic with toile fabric bordered by gimp trim.

You'll be enlightened when you discover how simple it is to beautify lamps with self-adhesive lampshades, fabric, and an array of trims. Add a personal touch to the tabletop of a wine rack by sheathing it in a distinctive fabric. A planter or basket makes a great decorative accent when adorned with toile and tassels. Anchor the room with a well-traveled trunk. Topped with toile fabric, it seems to have a story all its own.

**TIP** Trunks make great coffee tables — and they add bonus storage to your room! Place glass on top to create a bigger surface, or stack smaller trunks for an end table.

**Supplies**
- bench (ours measures 32"x35"x17")
- 3½" thick foam
- fabric
- hot glue gun
- tassel trim

**Techniques You'll Need**
- Bonding with Glue (p. 77)

1. Measure the length and width of the top of your bench between the uprights; cut a piece of foam this size.
2. Draw around foam on wrong side of fabric; cut out fabric 20" outside drawn lines.
3. Place foam on wrong side of fabric. Folding fabric like a package, glue excess fabric to back of foam.
4. Glue tassel trim around top edge of foam.

**TIP** To cut through thick pieces of foam quickly and easily, use an electric knife.

**Supplies**
- ⅞"w fusible web tape
- 26"x28" fabric piece
- hot glue gun
- two 12" lengths of 6" bullion fringe
- polyester batting
- 21"x26" coordinating fabric piece
- 4" tall ecru dyeable monogram letters to spell PARIS
- fabric dye (if desired)
- 1⅞ yds gimp trim

**Techniques You'll Need**
- Fusing Basics (p. 72)
- Single Hem (p. 76)
- Bonding with Glue (p. 77)

*Note: We dyed our ecru monogram letters black to coordinate with our fabrics.*

1. Make a 1" single hem along short edges of fabric piece.
2. With right side of fabric facing up, fuse web tape along long edges of fabric piece; remove paper backing.
3. Matching right sides and long edges, fold fabric in half and fuse edges in place. Turn pillow right side out.
4. With seam at center back, glue one length of fringe inside one side edge of pillow. Glue this side of pillow closed.
5. Stuff pillow with batting to desired fullness. Repeat Step 4 on other side of pillow.
6. For sash, make a 1" single hem along long edges and one short edge of coordinating fabric piece.
7. Overlapping short edges with hemmed edge on top, wrap sash around pillow and glue in place along short edges.
8. If desired, follow dye manufacturer's instructions to dye monogram letters; allow to dry. Glue letters to pillow to form word.
9. Wrapping ends to back of sash, glue lengths of gimp trim above and below word. Overlapping ends at back of pillow, glue a length of gimp trim on each side of word.

### Supplies
- scenic tapestry fabric
- $^7/_8$"w fusible web tape
- coordinating tapestry fabric
- hot glue gun
- decorative rod with finials and hardware

### Techniques You'll Need
- Fusing Basics (p. 72)
- Single Hem (p. 76)
- Bonding with Glue (p. 77)

1. Leaving 1" extra on each side of borders, cut out scene in tapestry.
2. Make a 1" single hem on each side of tapestry.

3. For tabs, cut five 6"x9" strips from coordinating fabric. Make a 1" single hem along long edges of each tab. Matching ends, fold each tab in half; glue ends together to form a loop.
4. Evenly space tabs along top back of tapestry and glue in place.
5. Mount rod on wall; slide tabs onto rod.

### Supplies
- stool with padded seat
- fabric
- staple gun
- T-pins
- hot glue gun
- tassel trim
- gimp trim

### Techniques You'll Need
- Bonding with Glue (p. 77)

1. Turn stool upside down. Draw around seat of stool on wrong side of fabric. Cut fabric 3" outside drawn line.
2. Center seat of stool on cut fabric, then pulling the fabric taut, staple opposite edges of the fabric to the bottom of the seat. Working on opposite sides of the seat and stapling as you go, stretch the fabric evenly around the seat, folding the fabric to ease in place. If necessary, trim excess fabric from the bottom of the seat.
3. Using T-pins to hold trim in place as you go, glue tassel trim along the bottom edge of the seat, then glue gimp along the top of the tassel trim. Remove T-pins.

**TIP** We used the wrong side of the fabric for a unique look on our stool (photo 1). It easily coordinates with the pillow, which uses the right side of the fabric (photo 2).

## TOILE MAGAZINE RACK

*from page 65*

### Supplies
- kraft paper
- fusible web
- magazine rack
- fabric
- pressing cloth
- craft glue
- gimp trim

### Techniques You'll Need
- Fusing Basics (p. 72)
- Bonding with Glue (p. 77)

1. Cut pattern from kraft paper slightly smaller than side of magazine rack. Trace around pattern twice on fusible web.
2. Centering design as desired, iron each fusible web piece to fabric; cut out. Remove paper backing on both pieces.
3. Use pressing cloth and fuse one fabric piece to each side of magazine rack.
4. Glue trim along edges of fabric pieces.

**TIP** If your magazine rack is not symmetrical, mark an "X" on your kraft paper as you draw your pattern. With "X" side of paper down, trace pattern onto fusible web.

## CHANDELIER TABLE LAMP

*from page 66*

### Supplies
- self-adhesive lampshade kits to fit lamp
- fabric
- craft glue
- tassel trim
- clothespins
- gimp trim
- chandelier-style table lamp

### Techniques You'll Need
- Bonding with Glue (p. 77)

Use clothespins to secure trims on lampshades until glue is dry.

1. Follow manufacturer's instructions to cover lampshades with fabric.
2. Glue tassel trim along bottom edge of each shade.
3. Glue gimp trim above tassel trim along bottom edge of each shade. Glue gimp trim along top edge of each shade.
4. Attach shades to lamp.

**TIP** Lampshades are a great way to express your creativity. With the abundance of trims available, from beads to feathers, you can create a one-of-a-kind designer look in minutes.

## UPDATED PLANTER

*from page 66*

**Supplies**
- planter or basket
- fabric
- $^7/_8$"w fusible web tape
- hot glue gun
- tassel trim

**Techniques You'll Need**
- Fusing Basics (p. 72)
- Single Hem (p. 76)
- Bonding with Glue (p. 77)

1. For fabric wrap, measure around planter; add 2". Measure desired height for fabric on planter; add 2". Cut a piece of fabric the determined measurements.

2. Make a 1" single hem on both long edges and one short edge of fabric.
3. Overlapping short edges with hemmed edge on top, wrap and glue fabric around container.
4. Glue tassel trim along top edge of fabric.

## WINE RACK TABLE

*from page 66*

**Supplies**
- wine rack with tabletop
- fabric
- staple gun

1. Turn wine rack upside down. Draw around top of wine rack on wrong side of fabric; cut out fabric 3" outside drawn lines.

2. Smooth fabric over top of wine rack, then wrap and staple opposite edges of fabric to the bottom of the tabletop. Working on opposite sides of the tabletop and stapling in place as you go, smooth the fabric evenly around the tabletop; trim excess fabric from the bottom.

**TIP** To protect the fabric, we had a small piece of glass cut slightly larger than the tabletop. Inexpensive and worth it!

## OLD WORLD TRUNK

*from page 67*

**Supplies**
- fabric
- antique trunk
- spray adhesive
- craft glue
- gimp trim

**Techniques You'll Need**
- Bonding with Glue (p. 77)

1. Centering design as desired, cut a piece of fabric to fit top of trunk.
2. Use spray adhesive to adhere fabric to top of trunk.
3. Glue gimp along raw edges of fabric.

**TIP** If you are really adventurous, try covering the entire trunk the same way you did the top. You can even mix and match different fabrics for a really coordinated look.

# fusing basics

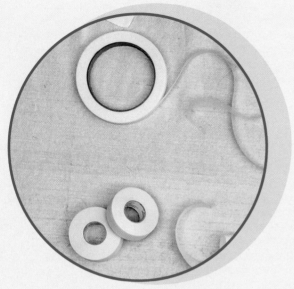

Paper-backed fusible web tape comes on a roll in a variety of widths. It is great for hemming, joining fabric widths, and fusing ribbons to fabrics. For almost all of our projects, we used the 7/8" wide tape for a perfect 1" hem.

There are two kinds of fusible web, basic paper-backed web and repositionable single or double-sided sticky fusible web. Repositionable web (Steam-A-Seam) has a temporary hold until you iron it in place.

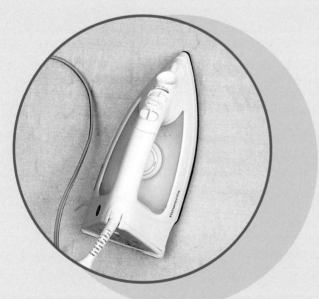

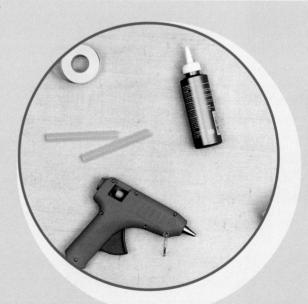

Iron is used to activate fusible adhesives to join two fabrics together.

Using hot glue is a quick and easy way to add decorative trims to projects. Craft glue takes a little longer to dry, but works best for layering trims on projects.

TIP  Basic paper-backed web and web tape come in several weights. The heavy-duty or ultra-web is best for medium to heavy-weight fabrics such as home décor and upholstery fabric. Lightweight webs work well with light or sheer fabrics. We used the heavy-duty web for most of the projects in this book.

Using fusible web has become the timesaving alternative to sewing! Everyone from the beginning crafter to the most experienced designer can appreciate the ease and simplicity of this no-sew method.

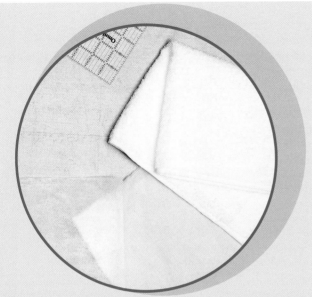

A **fusible work surface** can be an ironing board or a towel covered with silver ironing board fabric. A **pressing cloth** (such as muslin) protects the project's surface.

A **rotary cutter**, **clear quilting/crafting ruler**, and a **cutting mat** make cutting straight edges easy. The **cutting mat** protects the work surface.

**Craft fusible interfacing** is a dense fusible interfacing with more adhesive than regular fusible interfacing.

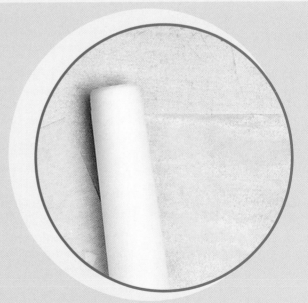

**Fusible interfacing** (typically used for sewing) is a lightweight interfacing with a bit of fusible adhesive on one side. It adds a little flexible stability to a project.

## FUSIBLE PRODUCTS

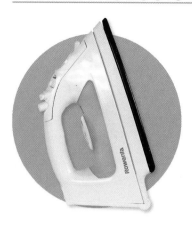

Fusible web is an adhesive that's activated by the heat of an iron. We have used paper-backed fusible products throughout this book, as they are easier to work with. Once the web is ironed onto the back of the fabric, the paper backing is peeled off, and the fabric is ready to be ironed in place. It's ideal for appliqués, hemming, and joining fabric pieces together. There are lots of brands of fusible web on the market.

As for any product, following the manufacturer's instructions will ensure a sufficient bond, but since you will be using many decorator fabrics, we recommend that you follow the fabric laundering instructions to determine if you should pre-wash fabrics before you begin. Fusible products require different combinations of heat, moisture, and pressure to adhere the two fabrics together. When you use double the adhesive you double the strength of the bond — you do this by fusing web or web tape to both side of the fabrics that are to be joined. If in doubt, test the fusible product on a scrap of fabric before making your project.

For simplifying home decorating projects, paper-backed fusible web couldn't be better! Not only does it hold projects together securely, you can create the straightest seams ever! it also gives them the appearance of a professional finish. Never has creating a roomful of fashionable accessories been so easy.

Don't sew a seam, fuse it!

## WORK SURFACE FOR FUSING

To avoid getting adhesive on your ironing board, wrap it in a scrap piece of batting and a piece of ironing board cover fabric before beginning. (You can find this silver-coated fabric at most fabric stores.) Use safety pins to secure the pieces beneath the board for a snug fit and a stable surface. If you do get fusible adhesive on your ironing board cover, place a scrap piece of fabric over the area and iron over it — the web will transfer to the fabric. Repeat with a new scrap until all the web has been removed.

For projects that are too large to manipulate on an ironing board, it's simple to create a larger ironing surface. Arrange a large, thick, towel, blanket, or comforter on a large table or the floor, then cover it with ironing board cover fabric.

Use a scrap piece of muslin or cotton for a pressing cloth to protect the iron when working with fusibles. If the adhesive gets onto your iron, use an iron cleaning product to remove it.

*For more information on fusing, see decorative accents chapter introductions, beginning on page 88.*

## BASIC FUSING - web sheets

**Supplies**
- iron
- fusible web
- fabric (from project instructions)

**Techniques You'll Need**
- Fusing Basics (p. 72)
- Work Surface for Fusing (p. 74)

*Prepare a Work Surface for Fusing (opposite page) and gather all necessary supplies before fusing.*

1. Set your iron to the temperature for your fabric and fusible web.
2. Place adhesive side of fusible web on wrong side of fabric to be fused. Press evenly over the entire piece for a strong bond (photo 1); let cool.
3. Remove paper backing.
4. Position fusible fabric, web side down, on project.
5. Press to fuse pieces together (photo 2).

## BASIC FUSING - web tape

**Supplies**
- iron
- fusible web tape (width from project instructions)
- ribbon or trim (from project instructions)

**Techniques You'll Need**
- Fusing Basics (p. 72)
- Work Surface for Fusing (p. 74)

*Prepare a Work Surface for Fusing (opposite page) and gather all necessary supplies before fusing.*

1. Set your iron to the temperature for your fabric and fusible web.
2. Place adhesive side of fusible web tape on wrong side of ribbon or trim to be fused. Press evenly over the entire piece for a strong bond (photo 1); let cool.
3. Remove paper backing.
4. Position fusible item, web side down, on project.
5. Press to fuse pieces together (photo 2).

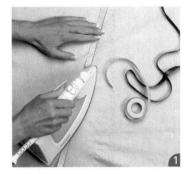
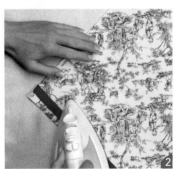

# SINGLE HEM

### Supplies
- fusible web tape (width from project instructions)
- iron
- fabric (from project instructions)

### Techniques You'll Need
- Fusing Basics (p. 72)

*If the selvage edge of your fabric is puckered, clip the selvage at 2" to 3" intervals and press flat (or trim off).*

1. Refer to photo 1 to fuse web tape along hem edge on the wrong side of your fabric (the width of the tape you'll need will be indicated in project instructions).
2. Press the edge to the wrong side and fuse in place (photo 2).

# MAKING FABRIC TRIM

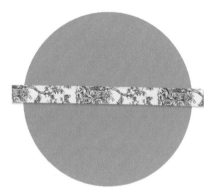

### Supplies
- fusible web tape
- fabric strip (from project instructions)

### Techniques You'll Need
- Fusing Basics (p. 72)

*We suggest using lightweight to medium weight fabrics for fabric trim — cotton works best. Cutting your fabric strip on the bias allows it to stretch and go around curves.*

### Hemmed Fabric Trim
1. With long raw edges meeting at back, press the fabric strip; unfold strip, then fuse web tape along each long edge on wrong side of fabric strip (photo 1). Remove the paper backing, refold strip and fuse in place.
2. Fuse lengths of web tape along edges on wrong side of trim (photo 2). Remove paper backing and fuse to project. (Fabric trim; photo 3.)

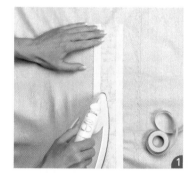

# MITERING CORNERS

**Supplies**
- fabric (from project instructions)
- scissors or rotary cutter and cutting mat
- iron
- $1/2$"w fusible web tape

**Techniques You'll Need**
- Fusing Basics (p. 72)

1. Cut corners from fabric as shown in photo 1.
2. Press one short edge of fabric in place as shown in photo 2. Repeat with remaining short edge.
3. Press one corner of one long edge of fabric diagonally to wrong side as shown in photo 3. Repeat with remaining corners.
4. Fuse a piece of web tape along diagonal edge as shown in photo 4.
5. Repeat Step 4 for remaining corners. Fuse each long edge of fabric piece in place.

# BONDING WITH GLUE

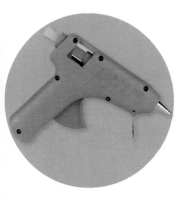

*Always follow the glue manufacturer's instructions for best results.*

We used hot glue for most of our finishing touches. It's quick and easy to use and provides immediate results.

We do not recommend the cool melt glues, as they cool too fast and do not create the best bonding results.

Use a craft stick or the tip of the glue gun to press the glue into your fabric. This also prevents burnt fingers.

When using hot glue, apply the glue in a manageable length. For instance, apply a bead of glue 12" along the fabric edge; place trim along glue, straighten and press in place, then move to the next 12" along the fabric edge.

Thick craft glue and fabric glue can be used to bond fabrics and other textiles, such as layering trims together. Use an even coat, spreading the glue with a craft stick, paintbrush, or your fingers.

To use spray adhesive, place ribbon, lace or fabric wrong side up on a scrap piece of cardboard or heavy-duty foil. Spray, pull up, and stick in place.

**TIP** Use clothespins or straight pins to hold glued items in place until the glue has dried completely.

# knife-edge
## PILLOWS

*It doesn't get any easier than this: Remove the need for sewing, and you've got a handsome home accent that practically creates itself. Add quick embellishments, and your pillow radiates fashion from every angle. It looks like a pricey purchase — but you made it in just minutes!*

When you just need a quick change of color on your favorite chair or sofa, create a basic knife-edge pillow (opposite). Want a little more visual interest? Add a sash (left) of coordinating fabric, cherry-red ribbon and a big, bold button. Your pillow is now a treat to behold.

**TIP** The secret to an iron-clad fusible bond is in layering your fusible products. For instance, by using fusible web tape on each of the two fabric pieces that form a knife-edge pillow, you'll double the strength of your seam.

# knife-edge PILLOWS

Want to dress up a plain pillow you already have, or perhaps give your basic knife-edge pillow a little more panache? Tie on beribboned squares (above). Fusible web and fabric glue make this "no-sew" easy to complete! For a different view, fashion the same fabric, ribbon, and buttons into an easy grid to make a windowpane pillow (opposite).

# envelope
## PILLOWS

*What's all the flap about? Eye appeal — and lots of it! A knife-edge pillow becomes an elegant envelope when you add a simple flap of fabric and posh embellishments. Whether you prefer dangling beads or tasseled trim, you can create a pretty pillow and never sew a single stitch.*

Sign them and seal them if you wish, but you'll never want to send these envelopes away: A seemingly eccentric mix of prints — roses, leopard, and stripes — creates a basic flap pillow (opposite) that's right in any room. And don't overlook the remnant table when shopping for fabric — a leftover piece of medallion print fabric was consigned to the scrap pile before it became the crowning touch on this envelope flap pillow (left).

**TIP** There are a wealth of trims available, from elegant beads to tasseled trim. Sometimes they get a little pricey, but these pillows only use $1/2$ to $3/4$ yard of trim. Splurge! A little bit goes a long way towards that elegant decorator look.

# flange
## PILLOWS

*The flange pillow is a simple design that's an especially good way to display large-print fabrics. This is because the flat edge can form a backdrop for trims, or it can be used as a coordinating border to draw the eye to the center of the pillow.*

Lace trim is all a simple open-edge flange pillow (opposite) needs to complement its provincial rose print. The ornate fabric used to create the blue and yellow flange pillow (left) lends itself to bolder embellishments — flat trim inside the flange and rope cording in the outer "seam."

**TIP** When fusing, never slide your iron. Press firmly, then move your iron by lifting it straight up and setting it straight down. This will keep your fabric layers even while creating a smooth finish.

# accent
## PILLOWS

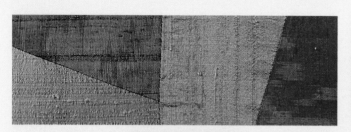

*Anything's possible! With all the fabrics and embellishments available to you, there must be thousands of original pillows you could create. So make as many of these cozy decorator accessories as you wish. When they're this quick to finish, you've got the time.*

The patchwork pillow appears to be a time-consuming creation — but it isn't. We used pre-sewn patchwork fabric to make this comfy cushion. And texture is another way to get great looks with just a little effort. The richness of tapestry fabric lends a little more luxury to this tasseled neck-roll pillow.

**TIP** You can create pillows of any dimension you desire by changing the measurements we have given. For example, the neck-roll pillow above could be made into a body pillow.

## Supplies
- two 20" squares of fabric (for an 18" finished pillow)
- $7/8$"w fusible web tape
- polyester batting

## Techniques You'll Need
- Fusing Basics (p. 72)

*Before cutting the fabric squares for your pillow, determine if there is a pattern or design in your fabric that you want centered on your pillow (on one or both sides), such as a scene on toile fabric.*

1. With right sides of fabric squares facing up, fuse web tape along the top and bottom edges of each square; fuse tape along side edges of each square between the first strips of tape (do not overlap tape): photo 1.
2. Remove paper backing from tape on top and sides on each square; remove backing from tape on bottom edges in photo 2, to leave an opening for turning and stuffing.
3. Matching bottom edges, place fabric squares right sides together and fuse edges in place (do not iron over bottom edge where paper backing is still present).
4. Place pillow cover on work surface with opening at bottom. Finger press top right corner along side seam, creasing as shown in photo 3.
5. Finger press corner along top seam, creasing over side seam as shown in photo 4. Use a dot of glue to hold corner in place.
6. Always pressing to the same side, repeat Steps 4 and 5 for remaining corners.
7. For each perfectly crisp corner, refer to photo 5 to grasp corner with thumb and index finger; holding corner firmly, turn and push corner to right side.
8. Filling the corners first, stuff pillow with batting.
9. Remove paper backing from bottom edges of pillow; carefully fuse opening closed (photo 6).

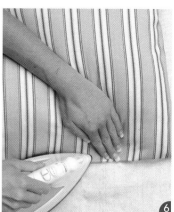

# SASH-WRAPPED PILLOW

*from page 79*

**Supplies**
- 7/8" and 1/2"w fusible web tape
- 17"x36" coordinating fabric piece for sash
- fusible web
- four 13" lengths of 5/8"w grosgrain ribbon
- 18" Basic Knife-Edge Pillow (p. 88)
- hot glue gun
- embroidery floss
- large button

**Techniques You'll Need**
- Fusing Basics (p. 72)
- Bonding with Glue (p. 77)

1. Make a 1" single hem along long edges of fabric piece.
2. Referring to photo 1, use fusible web to fuse each end of fabric piece in a point.
3. Fuse 1/2"w web tape along center on wrong sides of ribbon lengths. Wrapping ends to wrong side, fuse ribbon to points of sash.
4. Overlapping points, wrap sash around pillow and glue in place.

5. Knotting at back, thread embroidery floss through holes in button. Glue button to points; glue points to pillow to secure.

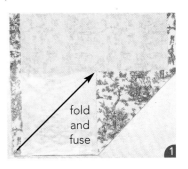

fold and fuse

1

# BERIBBONED SQUARES PILLOW

*from page 80*

**Supplies**
- 7/8"w fusible web tape
- two 14"x17" fabric pieces for pinafores
- eight 16" lengths of 7/8"w grosgrain ribbon
- hot glue gun
- embroidery floss
- eight large buttons
- 18" Basic Knife-Edge Pillow (p. 88)

**Techniques You'll Need**
- Fusing Basics (p. 72)
- Single Hem (p. 76)
- Bonding with Glue (p. 77)

1. Make a 1" single hem along edges of each fabric piece.
2. For each ribbon tie, glue one end of one ribbon length 1" to wrong side. Matching placement so ribbons line up on squares, glue folded ribbon ends to right sides of squares.
3. Knotting at back, thread embroidery floss through holes in each button. Glue buttons over ends of ribbons on squares.
4. Place pillow between squares; tie matching ribbon ends into bows and notch ends.

**TIP** Use two different, coordinating fabrics for the squares … giving you a fresh look when the pillow is turned over!

# WINDOWPANE PILLOW

*from page 81*

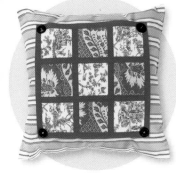

**Supplies**
- fusible web
- 8" square and 8"x12" coordinating fabrics for windowpane
- rotary cutter and cutting mat
- 12 1/2" solid-color fabric square for backing
- 1/2"w fusible web tape
- four 12 1/2" and four 14" lengths of 5/8"w grosgrain ribbon
- embroidery floss
- four large buttons
- hot glue gun
- 18" Basic Knife-Edge Pillow (p. 88)

**Techniques You'll Need**
- Fusing Basics (p. 72)
- Bonding with Glue (p. 77)

1. Fuse web to wrong sides of fabric pieces for windowpane.
2. Cut five 4" squares from the 8"x12" fabric piece and four 4" squares from the 8" fabric square; remove paper backing from squares.
3. Beginning with one of the five 4" squares at the center of the backing fabric and referring to photo, fuse 4" squares in place.

4. Fuse 1/2"w web tape along center on wrong sides of ribbon lengths. Referring to photo, center and fuse 12 1/2" ribbon lengths along "seams." Wrapping ends to back, fuse 14" ribbon lengths along edges of fused squares to complete windowpane.
5. Knotting at back, thread embroidery floss through holes in each button. Glue buttons at corners of windowpane. Glue corners of windowpane to front of pillow.

## BASIC FLAP PILLOW

*from page 82*

### Supplies
- $7/8$"w fusible web tape
- 5"x20" (bottom) and 8"x20" (top) coordinating fabric pieces for flap
- tacky glue
- 20" length of beaded trim with a ribbon flange
- hot glue gun
- 18" Basic Knife-Edge Pillow (p. 88)

### Techniques You'll Need
- Fusing Basics (p. 72)
- Single Hem (p. 76)
- Bonding with Glue (p. 77)

1. For flap, fuse web tape along one long edge on wrong side of bottom flap fabric piece and on right side of top flap fabric piece. Overlapping fused edges, fuse bottom piece to top piece.
2. Make a 1" single hem along top and side edges of combined 12"x20" fabric piece. Fold bottom fabric of flap in half to wrong side, and fuse in place.

3. Use tacky glue to adhere flange of trim along raw edges and ends to back of flap.
4. Hot glue top edge of flap along top edge of pillow.

## ENVELOPE FLAP PILLOW

*from page 83*

### Supplies
- fusible interfacing
- $14^1/2$"x18" coordinating fabric piece for envelope
- $7/8$"w fusible web tape
- hot glue gun
- $1^1/4$ yds of $1^1/4$" loop fringe trim with tassels
- $1^1/4$ yds of $1^1/4$" loop fringe trim
- 2" dia. button
- 4" dia. circle of fabric to cover button
- 18" Basic Knife-Edge Pillow (p. 88)

### Techniques You'll Need
- Fusing Basics (p. 72)
- Single Hem (p. 76)
- Bonding with Glue (p. 77)

*Before cutting the fabric square for your envelope flap, determine the placement of the pattern or design in your fabric that you want centered on your flap, such as the scene we used from our toile fabric (left).*

1. (**Note:** 18" edges are top and bottom of fabric piece.) Fuse interfacing to wrong side of fabric piece. Leaving 1" at top for hem, draw shape for flap on interfacing; cut out.
2. Make a 1" single hem along top edge of flap.

3. Referring to photo at left and wrapping and gluing ends of trim to top back of flap, glue tassel trim along raw edges of flap; repeat to glue loop trim along top edges of tassel trim.
4. Gluing ends to back, cover button with fabric. Beginning and ending at bottom and gluing on the backside, glue a length of loop trim to button. Glue a single tassel cut from the tassel trim to the bottom of the button, covering the loop trim ends.
5. Glue top edge of flap to top edge of pillow.
6. Glue button to flap and flap to pillow to secure in place.

## BASIC FLANGE PILLOW

*from page 84*

### Supplies
- fusible web
- two 24" squares of fabric (for a 20" finished pillow)
- embroidery floss to match pillow fabric
- polyester batting
- hot glue gun
- decorative trim

### Techniques You'll Need
- Fusing Basics (p. 72)
- Mitering Corners (p. 77)
- Bonding with Glue (p. 77)

1. Using 4" wide strips of fusible web and following Mitering Corners, make a 4" hem along edges of fabric squares.
2. Lightly mark a 10" square at center on right side of one fabric square. Pin fabric squares wrong sides together. Leaving an opening for stuffing, work a loose running stitch along drawn lines to attach fabric squares together.

3. Stuff pillow with batting to desired fullness; complete running stitch along marked line to close opening.
4. Beginning and ending at center bottom, glue trim over stitching, mitering or gently bending trim at corners.

# CORDED-EDGE FLANGE PILLOW

*from page 85*

**Supplies**
- fusible web
- two 24" squares of fabric (for an approx. 20" finished pillow)
- 15" fabric square for pillow center
- embroidery floss
- polyester batting
- hot glue gun
- flat trim
- cording with flange

**Techniques You'll Need**
- Fusing Basics (p. 72)
- Mitering Corners (p. 77)
- Bonding with Glue (p. 77)

1. Using 2" wide strips of fusible web and following Mitering Corners, make a 2" hem along edges of fabric squares.
2. Fuse 15" fabric square to center on right side of one fabric square.
3. Pin pillow squares wrong sides together. Leaving an opening for stuffing, work a running stitch just outside edges of pillow center to attach pillow squares together.

4. Stuff pillow with batting to desired fullness; complete running stitch along pillow center to close opening.
5. Beginning and ending at center bottom and mitering trim at corners, glue trim over stitching.
6. Beginning and ending at center bottom, glue flange of cording between edges of pillow.

# NECK-ROLL PILLOW

*from page 87*

**Supplies**
- $7/8$"w fusible web tape
- 19"x26" fabric piece
- 26" length of cording
- two 8" lengths of 4" bullion fringe
- polyester batting
- hot glue gun
- large tassel

**Techniques You'll Need**
- Fusing Basics (p. 72)
- Single Hem (p. 76)
- Bonding with Glue (p. 77)

1. Make a 1" single hem along short edges of fabric piece.
2. With right sides of fabric facing up, fuse web tape along long edges of fabric piece; remove paper backing.
3. Matching right sides and long edges, fold fabric in half and fuse edges in place. Turn pillow right side out.
4. With seam at center back, glue one end of cord inside top corner on one side and one length of fringe inside same side edge of pillow. Glue this side of pillow closed.

5. Stuff pillow with batting to desired fullness. Running the cord along the top edge of pillow for length, repeat Step 4 on other side of pillow.
6. Wrap and glue tassel hanger around center of cord; trim hanger of tassel as necessary.

# PATCHWORK KNIFE-EDGE PILLOW

*from page 86*

**Supplies**
- two 20" squares of pre-pieced fabric (for an 18" finished pillow)
- $7/8$"w fusible web tape
- polyester batting

**Techniques You'll Need**
- Fusing Basics (p. 72)

Make a Basic Knife-Edge Pillow, page 88, using fabric that is pre-pieced, giving it that handmade look that only you know was "simple-as-pie" to make!

**TIP** Be careful when fusing web to specialty fabrics, such as raw silk. Use a pressing cloth and possibly lower your iron temperature, as the heat of the iron can scorch the fabric. You may want to test your fusible product on a scrap of fabric first.

# floor
## COVERINGS

*Cover your floor in color and comfort with a fabulous floor cloth! Whether used to define a seating area or to embellish an entryway, rugs are warm and inviting. Choose tapestries or other heavy-weight fabrics to enhance your décor; then add borders or trims to suit your personal style.*

Often referred to as the "fifth wall," floors deserve attention when you're decorating. Area rugs can add the finishing touch to a hallway space or can be used to anchor a grouping of furniture together in a large room. Let yourself go wild and unleash your décor's potential by creating a leopard print-bordered floral floor cloth (opposite). Layering the floor in richness, this tapestry rug (left) is a cinch to fashion using bullion fringe to trim the ends.

**TIP** Use a fringe with looped ends instead of cut ends to prevent fraying.

**TIP** To keep your floor covering in place, paint the back with non-skid rug backing from a craft or home improvement store.

Welcome family and friends into your home with a tailor-made tapestry floor cloth. The bold floral print exudes a hint of Victorian elegance, while the generous border balances out the design.

# MITERED-BORDER RUG

*from page 92*

**Supplies**
- two coordinating tapestry fabrics
- heavy-duty fusible web
- ⁷⁄₈"w fusible tape

**Fusing Techniques**
- Fusing Basics (p. 72)
- Single Hem (p. 76)
- Mitering Corners (p. 77)

1. Cut a 4'x6' piece of fabric for floor cloth.
2. Cut two 10"x48" and two 10"x72" borders from coordinating fabric.
3. Make a 1" single hem along edges of each border. Press in half with wrong sides and long edges together.

4. Fuse heavy-duty fusible web to wrong side of each border.
5. Overlap and fuse short borders onto each end of rug.
6. Follow Steps 3 and 4 of Mitering Corners, page 77, to overlap and fuse long borders onto each long edge of rug.

# FRINGED FLOOR COVER

*from page 93*

**Supplies**
- heavy-weight fabric
- fusible web
- hot glue gun
- 3¹⁄₂" long bullion fringe

**Fusing Techniques**
- Fusing Basics (p. 72)
- Single Hem (p. 76)
- Bonding with Glue (p. 77)

1. Cut fabric to desired size for floor cover (ours measures 48"x76").
2. Make a 2" single hem along each long edge.
3. Glue fringe along each short edge.

# BORDERED FLOOR CLOTH

*from page 94*

**Supplies**
- tapestry fabric
- fusible web

**Fusing Techniques**
- Fusing Basics (p. 72)
- Single Hem (p. 76)

1. Leaving an extra 2" on each side, cut out tapestry design with borders (ours measures 26"x36").
2. Measure one short edge of cut fabric; add 2". Add 2" to border width on fabric; centering border design, cut two border strips.
3. Make a 1" single hem along each long edge of border strips.
4. Wrapping and fusing ends to back, overlap and fuse one border strip onto each short edge of tapestry design.

 **TIP** We used a tapestry fabric with a border along the edges. You can also buy a tapestry fabric and coordinating striped fabric – cut the stripes to use as the border fabric with the tapestry fabric in the center.

# toile
## PLACEMATS

*The indispensable placemat protects your table while adding color and style to mealtimes. As with all no-sew designs, your placemats can be formal, fun, or something in between. So let your favorite fabric set the pace while you set each place at the table.*

Toile makes any place setting look absolutely delicious. Today's toile comes in so many colors you're sure to find the perfect pattern to coordinate with your most treasured place settings.

**TIP** These placemats are actually reversible since the backing fabric is wrapped around to the front. Turn them over for a fresh new look!

# vinyl
## PLACEMATS

*If you like your decorative accessories to have a practical side, you'll love the duality of these pleasing placemats. Fabric fused to ready-made canvas sheets are sealed with iron-on vinyl that makes cleanup easy, while the fun fabrics make them perfect for all occasions. Put the fun in functional!*

Mealtime mishaps are no match for these festive table covers. Simply wipe them down with a damp cloth and they're ready to be used again.

**TIP** Browse through bolts of specialty print cotton fabrics in lieu of rolls of decorator fabrics. They feature hobbies, holidays, and other fun designs. Make placemats for year-round ... perfect for gift-giving, too!

# sheer
## TABLE TOPPERS

*A subtle addition to a breakfast nook or bedside table, these sheer fabric coverings breathe new life into a room. With a look reminiscent of vintage linens, the easy edges and satiny trims make these sheers a breeze.*

Whether it's summer florals or romantic lace you fancy, a sheer table topper in your favorite print can freshen the look of any table. The basic fabric width can be made into a square that will cover standard-size round tables without having to piece sections together.

**TIP** To avoid scorching, delicate satin ribbon and sheer fabric require a slightly cooler iron temperature. Also, use a "lite" fusible web product.

# round
## TABLE SKIRTS

*Small, round accent tables are staple furnishings in many rooms, but are often pushed into a corner merely to hold the treasures of days gone by. Transform these classic pieces into stylized displays by topping them with an engaging table skirt.*

A table skirt can call for a lot of fabric. Stay within budget by puddling inexpensive burlap (opposite) over the table, then topping it with an elegant damask table topper. Hemmed with fusible tape and embellished with cording, an understated fabric (left) enhances a side table without overpowering the decorative pieces displayed.

TIP Add extra storage space to any room by covering an easy-to-assemble, round table kit with a table skirt. The skirt conceals odds and ends that can clutter the room. Some of the larger diameter table kits even come with shelves built in.

103

# table
# RUNNERS

*Time-tested table runners and dresser scarves have added elegance and style to buffets, tables, and chests for centuries. Fresh fabrics and fabulous trims bring them up to date and the techniques are so easy, you'll be set for entertaining and decorating in no time at all.*

**TIP** Choosing striped fabrics for the table runners works especially well since they have ready-made "lines" to follow for cutting your fabric and fusing hems.

An elegant step up from the traditional placemat, beaded runners draped across the table (opposite) create an air of formal dining, while a runner atop a buffet (above) serves up colorful accents. A tasseled scarf over a chest (right) provides a protective yet decorative highlight.

# table cover THROW

*When it comes to decorating, think outside the box. Don't feel limited by the traditional uses of what you're creating. When choosing fabrics, think about how they can coordinate with other rooms in your home.*

Edged in bullion fringe, this elegant chenille fabric makes an effortless transition from table cover to soft sofa throw with no modifications required.

TIP Adding a bit of decorator fringe instead of hemming can dramatically transform the appearance of an ordinary topper or throw. A lush bullion fringe like this one adds pizzazz.

### Supplies
- ½ yd fabric
- ½ yd fusible vinyl
- fusible web
- 17½"x13½" canvas placemat (sold in packages of four)

### Techniques You'll Need
- Fusing Basics (p. 72)

*Iron-On Vinyl is a clear vinyl that has a fusible adhesive on one side and the paper backing is used as a pressing cloth. It comes in matte and glossy finishes. The vinyl makes the fabric resist water and scuffs and prevents it from stretching, making it perfect for placemats. It comes in 17" wide by 2-yard rolls.*

1. Cut fabric 20½"x16½"; cut vinyl 21"x17".
2. Fuse fabric to placemat, wrapping edges to back and folding like a package.

3. Follow manufacturer's instructions to fuse vinyl to placemat the same way as fabric.

**TIP** Use the paper backing from each placemat as its pressing cloth; using one sheet over and over burns off the coating on the paper, causing it to stick to the vinyl.

## TOILE PLACEMATS

### Supplies
- ½ yd toile fabric
- ½ yd coordinating fabric
- fusible interfacing
- fusible web
- ½"w fusible web tape
- fusible web tape (⅛" smaller than ribbon or gimp width)
- 1¼ yds grosgrain ribbon or gimp

### Techniques You'll Need
- Fusing Basics (p. 72)
- Mitering Corners (p. 77)

1. To center the fabric design for your placemat, cut a piece of fusible interfacing 19"x13". Working on the wrong side of your fabric, use the interfacing piece as a guide to place over the design area you wish to use, then fuse the interfacing in place.
2. Cut a 23"x17" rectangle of coordinating fabric.
3. Fuse web to wrong side of coordinating fabric; remove paper backing. Center and fuse toile fabric to wrong side of coordinating fabric.

4. Following Mitering Corners, fuse edges of coordinating fabric piece onto toile.
5. For ribbon or gimp trim, fuse web tape along center of ribbon or gimp; remove paper backing. For ribbon, cut one length to fit along each inner edge of placemat border, overlapping ends; fuse in place. For gimp, fuse entire length of gimp along inner edge of placemat border, gently bending around corners.

## MEASURING YOUR TABLE

To measure round tables for table skirts, refer to the Round Table Diagram. Measure the diameter of the table, then determine the drop length (the distance from the tabletop to the desired length). The size of a table skirt is the diameter of the table plus twice the drop length.

To measure a table for a table runner, refer to the Square Table Diagram. Measure the length and width of the table according to how you want your table runner to fit. You can also lay your uncut fabric on the table to help you decide on the right measurements for the look you want.

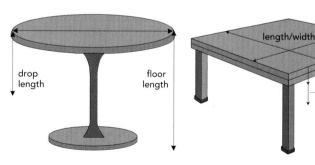

## JOINING FABRIC PANELS

Fused seams should be placed at the sides rather than at the center of your table skirt or topper. When joining two fabric panels for a skirt or topper, you'll need to use a full width of fabric at the center with a half width fused to each side. (When joining three full fabric panels, you'll need to use a full width of fabric at the center with a full width fused to each side.)

To join fabric panels, fuse ⁷/₈"w paper-backed fusible web tape along the seam edge on the right side of each fabric panel. Remove paper backing from tape. Place panels right sides together and fuse in place. Open panels and press along the "seamline"; the fused edge will look like a sewn seam.

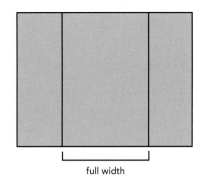

full width

**TIP** If your fabric has a repeating pattern, refer to Matching Prints, page 122, as you join your panels together.

## CUTTING A CIRCLE

Fold fabric from project instructions in half from top to bottom and again from left to right. Divide table measurement by two and add 1". Tape T-pin to yardstick at the 1" mark with point extending past bottom edge of yardstick. Tape a

fabric marker to yardstick at the determined measurement with point extending past bottom edge of yardstick. With T-pin at point where folds intersect, rotate yardstick to draw a circle on fabric with marker; cut out circle through all layers of fabric.

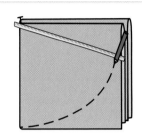

**TIP** If the diameter of your circle is larger than one fabric width, see Joining Fabric Panels, above, to make a larger square.

## SHEER WHITE TABLE TOPPER

*from page 101*

**Supplies**
- sheer white fabric
- ³/₄"w and ⁷/₈"w fusible web tape
- ⁵/₈"w satin ribbon

**Techniques You'll Need**
- Measuring Your Table (p. 108)
- Single Hem (p. 76)
- Fusing Basics (p. 72)

1. Measure your table to determine desired size of topper; add 2" for hem and cut from fabric. (Our topper is 49" square finished; we cut a 51" square.)
2. Make a 1" single hem along edges of fabric.

3. For trim, fuse ³/₄"w tape along center of ribbon. Wrapping ends to back, fuse a length of ribbon along each inner hem edge on right side of topper.

## SHEER FLORAL TABLE TOPPER

*from page 100*

**Supplies**
- sheer floral fabric
- ³/₄"w fusible web tape
- ⁷/₈"w coordinating satin ribbon

**Techniques You'll Need**
- Fusing Basics (p. 72)
- Measuring Your Table (p. 108)

1. Measure your table to determine desired size of topper; cut a square from fabric.
2. Fuse the web tape along the center of the ribbon. Wrapping ribbon ends to back, fuse a length of ribbon along each raw edge of floral fabric square.

## BURLAP SKIRT WITH DAMASK TOPPER

*from page 102*

**Supplies**
- ⁷/₈"w fusible web tape
- 50"w burlap fabric
- damask fabric

**Techniques You'll Need**
- Measuring Your Table (p. 108)
- Joining Fabric Panels (p. 109)
- Cutting A Circle (p. 109)
- Fusing Basics (p. 72)
- Single Hem (p. 76)

1. Measure your table; add 8" for a "puddled" hem.
2. Follow Joining Fabric Panels to determine the number of fabric widths you need, then join panel widths.
3. Cut a circle from fabric.
4. Place the skirt on the table; tuck edge of fabric under at the floor and arrange folds for a puddled effect.

5. For topper, measure your table to determine desired size of topper; add 2" for hem and cut from damask fabric. (Our topper is 54" square finished; we cut a 56" square.) Make a 1" single hem along each edge of fabric. Arrange topper on table skirt.

## WINDOWPANE PLAID SKIRT

*from page 103*

**Supplies**
- 54"w plaid fabric
- ⁷/₈"w fusible web tape
- hot glue gun
- cording with flange

**Techniques You'll Need**
- Measuring Your Table (p. 108)
- Joining Fabric Panels (p. 109)
- Cutting A Circle (p. 109)
- Fusing Basics (p. 72)
- Single Hem (p. 76)
- Bonding with Glue (p. 77)

1. Measure your table; add 2¹/₂" for corded hem.
2. Follow Joining Fabric Panels to determine the number of widths you need, then join panel widths.
3. Cut a circle from fabric.

4. Make a 1" single hem along outside of fabric circle.
5. Glue flange of cording along hem of table skirt so that cording shows at bottom of skirt.

## BEADED RUNNER

*from page 104*

**Supplies**
- damask fabric
- ⁷/₈"w fusible web tape
- fusible web
- hot glue gun
- beaded trim with flange

**Techniques You'll Need**
- Single Hem (p. 76)
- Fusing Basics (p. 72)
- Bonding with Glue (p. 77)

1. To determine the length of your placemat runner, measure across your table, edge to edge; add 2" for each drop length and 9¹/₂" for each "point" (23" total). Cut a 21" wide piece of fabric the determined length.

2. Make a 1" single hem along each long edge of the fabric piece.
3. For each end, fuse a 9¹/₂"x19" piece of web to wrong side, across end of fabric; remove paper backing. Using paper backing as a pressing cloth (shiny side down) fuse corners to a point (photo 1).
4. Press point 4³/₄" to center on wrong side of runner, forming a flat edge at end of runner (photo 2). Apply glue along edges on wrong side of point and refold in place.
5. Gently bending around the corners, glue flange of trim to wrong side along each edge of placemat runner.

**TIP** Cut a smaller fabric rectangle and finish both ends like we did on our table runner to create a fancy placemat.

## FRINGED RUNNER

*from page 105*

**Supplies**
- heavy-weight fabric
- $^7/_8$"w fusible web tape
- hot glue gun
- 4" bullion fringe

**Techniques You'll Need**
- Measuring Your Table (p. 108)
- Fusing Basics (p. 72)
- Single Hem (p. 76)
- Bonding with Glue (p. 77)

1. Measure your table to determine desired length and width of table runner. Subtract 8" from length for fringe and add 2" to width; cut fabric these dimensions.
2. Make a 1" single hem along each long edge of table runner.
3. Wrapping fringe ends to back, glue fringe along each end of table runner.

**TIP** If you want your fringe to hang over the edge of your table, measure the table drop length you want, then subtract 8" for the fringe length.

## TASSELED RUNNER

*from page 105*

**Supplies**
- heavy-weight fabric
- $^7/_8$"w fusible web tape
- hot glue gun
- $3^1/_2$" tassel trim

**Techniques You'll Need**
- Measuring Your Table (p. 108)
- Fusing Basics (p. 72)
- Single Hem (p. 76)
- Bonding with Glue (p. 77)

1. Measure your table to determine desired length and width of table runner. Subtract 7" from length for tassel trim and add 2" to width; cut fabric to these dimensions.
2. Make a 1" single hem along each long edge of the table runner.
3. Wrapping trim ends to back, glue trim along each end of table runner.

**TIP** Use plenty of glue when adhering heavy-weight fabrics and trim together. Use a craft stick to hold glued item in place and avoid burning your fingers.

## TABLE COVER THROW

*from page 106*

**Supplies**
- chenille fabric
- $^7/_8$"w fusible web tape
- hot glue gun
- $4^1/_2$" fringe trim

**Techniques You'll Need**
- Measuring Your Table (p. 108)
- Fusing Basics (p. 72)
- Single Hem (p. 76)
- Bonding with Glue (p. 77)

1. Measure your table if making a table topper.
2. Cut fabric desired size for throw or table topper.
3. Pressing fabric to the right side, make a 1" single hem along each edge of fabric.
4. With fringe extending beyone edge of fabric and gently bending it around corners, hot glue fringe to edge of fabric, making sure to cover the raw edge.

# delightful
## DRAPES

Shirred on a decorative rod, these delicately patterned panels are elegant whether draped or pulled back with a generous tasseled tie-back. Flowing into "puddles" along the floor, these opulent drapes are topped with a coordinating fabric and accentuated with shimmering beads.

*Don't miss this window of opportunity to dress your home in sophisticated style. Made from rich fabrics, these curtains provide a hint of formality.*

**TIP** This is the easiest gathered drape to make. The gathered top makes it easily adjustable to your window size. You can add as many panels as you want to the one rod to achieve the desired fullness.

# topped-off
## PANELS

*These curtains are not only beautiful, they're a sheer delight to make! Using our no-sew methods, it's a breeze to create these pretty panels.*

Satin ribbons suspend these lacy sheers as they dance gracefully in front of the windows. Silk roses add a touch of timeless romance. A fun alternative to traditional rod-pocket curtains, tab-top panels take shape quickly and offer a crisp, yet casual, look.

**TIP** Choosing a fabric with a scalloped border like the lace panels at left makes life easy. No side hems to fuse! If you allow for extra fabric to puddle curtains, there is no bottom hem either!

115

# dramatic
## DRAPE

*Curtains aren't just for windows! Flowing with texture, this regal drape graces a French door to lend an element of drama to the room.*

Hung from clip-on curtain rings, this drape is a cinch to make. Simply pair a solid fabric with a coordinating tapestry-look print and add a tassel trim along the seam. Pull it back with a large tasseled tie-back or let it fall free; either way, it's eye-catching!

TIP The rusty red fabric was found at a bargain on a "flat fold" table. With the extra savings there, you can splurge on a more expensive fabric for the lower part of the drapery since only a small amount of yardage is needed.

# captivating
## CORNICES

*Cornices add the crowning touch to a window. Constructed using foam cornice board kits, these window treatments are striking yet easy to make.*

Fanciful fringe accentuates the scalloped edges of an opulent topper which is sure to draw admiring glances. A blend of botanical and animal prints gives this cornice its natural appeal. Add softness to a window with a cornice-topped balloon valance. The graceful folds are made by drawing up the material with fabric strips embellished with tassels.

**TIP** If you have a larger window, two cornice boards can be joined together. Another added feature of the foam cornice boards is that they are lightweight and so easy to hang.

119

# eye-catching
## SHADES

*Window shades are an excellent decorating element, because they provide both beauty and privacy. And best of all, the design options are limitless.*

This delightful duo is both decorative and functional. Create it by covering a shade kit with your choice of fabric, and then top it with a complementary swag valance. Simply stunning, this balloon shade is an impressive addition to a room. Velvet ribbons gather the fabric into fashionable folds.

**TIP** If you would like the balloon shade to close for privacy, add hook-and-loop fasteners to the ends of the ribbon; connect ends together at top back of shade. It will be a "cinch" to "uncinch"!

# MEASURING YOUR WINDOW

Measure each window individually; windows may look the same but have slightly different measurements. Refer to diagram below to measure windows for different types of installation (inside or outside) and lengths (sill length, apron length, floor length) of window treatments. Mount curtain rod before measuring for length of window treatment.

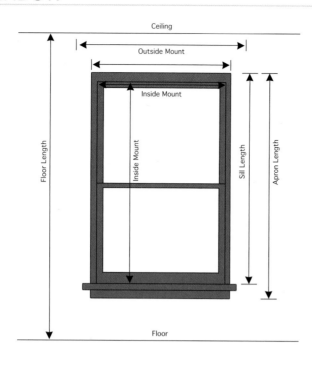

**TIP** Outside window mounts can help disguise problems with windows that are too narrow or are out of balance with the rest of your room. By placing rods almost to the ceiling and extending them well past the window moldings, you can make any window appear larger.

# MATCHING PRINTS

1. If selvage edges are puckered, clip selvages at 2" to 3" intervals and press.
2. Place panels right sides together, matching selvage edges. Beginning at one end of panels, fold top selvage edge back along edges to be joined until pattern on both panels matches (photo 1); press along fold. Use a fabric marking pen or pencil to mark bottom panel where pattern matches fold of top panel (photo 2).

3. For top panel, measure from fold and mark width of web tape along length of excess fabric. Trim fabric along marked line. Unfold edge and make a single hem along edge (see Single Hem, page 76).
4. On right side of bottom panel, fuse web tape next to drawn line (photo 3). Remove paper backing.

5. Lay panels right side up on a flat surface. Overlap hemmed edge of top panel over taped edge of bottom panel so that design repeats match. Fuse panels together.
6. For heavier fabrics, fuse web tape along wrong side of hemmed edge of top panel before fusing panels together.

# DAMASK CURTAIN

*from page 113*

**Supplies**
- decorative curtain rod with finials and mounting brackets
- fabric
- fusible web

**Techniques You'll Need**
- Measuring Your Window (p. 122)
- Fusing Basics (p. 72)
- Single Hem (p. 76)
- Joining Fabric Panels (p. 109)

1. Leaving 2" for header, follow manufacturer's instructions to hang curtain rod in window.
2. Measure window from top of rod to floor for curtain length; add 10". Measure between brackets for curtain width; add 4".
3. Cut a fabric panel the determined measurements. Make a 2" single hem on sides and bottom of panel.
4. For header, press top edge of panel 6" to wrong side. Cut two 2" wide strips of fusible web the width of the panel. Fuse one strip into the crease; fuse another along the raw edge to form rod pocket.
5. Thread panel onto curtain rod and hang.

# GOLD DRAPE WITH BEADED FRINGE

*from page 112*

**Supplies**
- decorative curtain rod with finials and mounting brackets
- solid fabric
- coordinating patterned fabric
- $7/8$"w fusible web tape
- hot glue gun
- beaded fringe
- fusible web

**Techniques You'll Need**
- Measuring Your Window (p. 122)
- Fusing Basics (p. 72)
- Single Hem (p. 76)
- Joining Fabric Panels (p. 109)

1. Leaving 3" for header, follow manufacturer's instructions to mount brackets and rod at desired position in window.
2. Measure window from top of rod to floor for panel length and between brackets for panel width.
3. For each panel, add 25" to length; cut solid fabric the determined measurements. Cut patterned fabric 25" by determined width.
4. Make a 1" single hem along one long edge of patterned fabric. Glue beaded fringe to wrong side of hem.
5. Cut a piece of fusible web the same size as patterned fabric; fuse to back and remove paper backing. Fuse patterned fabric onto top of solid fabric with beaded fringe between fabrics along one long edge.
6. Make a 1" single hem along each side of joined fabric pieces.
7. For header, cut one 3" wide strip of fusible web to equal the width of the panel. Press top of panel 7" to wrong side; unfold. Fuse web tape to wrong side along raw edge and fusible web strip along fold; remove paper backing, refold, and fuse in place.
8. Thread panels onto rod and hang. Tuck bottom edge of curtain under at the floor and arrange fabric for a "puddled" effect.

### Supplies
- decorative curtain rod with finials and mounting brackets
- solid fabric
- striped fabric
- $7/8$"w fusible web tape
- fabric glue
- tassel trim
- clip-on curtain rings

### Techniques You'll Need
- Measuring Your Window (p. 122)
- Fusing Basics (p. 72)
- Joining Fabric Panels (p. 109)
- Single Hem (p. 76)

1. Follow manufacturer's instructions to mount brackets and rod at desired position in window.
2. Measure window from top of rod to floor for curtain length and between brackets for curtain width. Divide length by three and multiply by two; add 9". Add 2" to width; cut a piece of solid fabric this size.
3. Divide length by three and add 2"; cut a piece of striped fabric this length and the same width as solid fabric.
4. Fuse web tape along one short edge on wrong side of solid fabric and on right side of striped fabric. Overlapping edges, fuse solid fabric to striped fabric.
5. Make a 1" single hem on bottom and both sides of drape.
6. For header, make a 4" single hem along top edge of drape. Fold again to make another 4" single hem.
7. Wrapping ends to back, glue tassel trim along seam between solid and striped fabrics.
8. Evenly space curtain rings along top of curtain. Thread rings onto rod and hang.

**TIP** Using clip-on rings makes it easy to slide the drapery back when the door is in use. Just remember to swag it to the hinged side of the door.

### Supplies
- decorative curtain rod with finials and mounting brackets
- lace fabric with scalloped selvages
- fusible web
- pressing cloth
- crochet needle
- $1/4$"w satin ribbon
- silk roses

### Techniques You'll Need
- Measuring Your Window (p. 122)
- Fusing Basics (p. 72)
- Single Hem (p. 76)

1. Follow manufacturer's instructions to mount brackets and rod at desired position.
2. Measure window from top of rod to floor for panel length; add $2^1/2$". For each panel, cut one selvage-to-selvage piece of lace fabric this size. The scalloped selvages will be the sides of the panel.
3. For header, cut a $2^1/2$" wide strip of fusible web. Using pressing cloth, fuse web along top edge of panel; press top edge of fabric $2^1/2$" to back so web is fused in the fold.
4. Make a 3" single hem along bottom edge of panel.
5. For tie holes, use crochet needle to carefully poke evenly spaced holes 2" from top of header. For each tie, thread a 30" length of ribbon through hole; bring ends of ribbon to top of header and tie in a knot. Tie ribbon into a bow 2" from ribbon ends.
6. Glue a silk rose over bottom of each tie.

**Supplies**
- decorative rod with finials and mounting brackets
- reversible fabric
- $^{7}/_{8}$"w fusible web tape
- fusible web
- hot glue gun
- tassel trim

**Techniques You'll Need**
- Measuring Your Window (p. 122)
- Fusing Basics (p. 72)
- Joining Fabric Panels (p. 109)
- Single Hem (p. 76)
- Fabric Trim (p. 76)

1. Follow manufacturer's instructions to mount brackets and rod at desired position in window.
2. Measure window from top of rod to floor for panel length and between brackets for panel width; add 5" to width and subtract 4" from length; cut a piece of fabric this size.
3. Make a 1" single hem along top and bottom and one side edge of panel.
4. Press remaining side of panel 4" to the right side (showing the reverse side of fabric). Fuse 4" wide strips of web along fold; remove paper backing and fuse in place.

5. Glue a length of trim along raw edge on front of panel.
6. To make each tab, cut a 12"x5" fabric strip and make fabric trim, following only Step 1 on p. 76.
7. Fold each tab in half; glue ends together. Spacing evenly, glue ends of tabs to top back of panel.
8. Slip tabs onto rod. Place rod in brackets; attach finials to ends of rod.

**Supplies**
- June Tailor® Deco-Wrap® No-Sew Cornice
- fabric
- hot glue gun
- tassel trim

**Techniques You'll Need**
- Measuring Your Window (p. 122)

1. Follow manufacturer's instructions to cut cornice board to fit in window if needed and wrap with fabric.
2. Glue trim along bottom edge of fabric.
3. Follow manufacturer's instructions to mount cornice board in window.

**TIP** Use the pattern in your fabric as a guide to create scallops along the edge of your fabric or draw around the edge of a plate or bowl to create scallops.

**Supplies**
- June Tailor® Deco-Wrap® No-Sew Cornice
- three coordinating fabrics
- $7/8$" dia. cotton cord
- $7/8$"w fusible web tape

**Techniques You'll Need**
- Measuring Your Window (p. 122)
- Fusing Basics (p. 72)

1. Follow manufacturer's instructions to cut cornice board to fit in window if needed and wrap with two fabrics.
2. To make welting, cut two $2^5/8$" wide bias strips of the remaining fabric, 2" longer than cornice board; cut two pieces of cord the same length.

3. Fuse web tape along one long edge on wrong side of each fabric strip. Lay cord down the middle of each strip. Remove paper backing; matching raw edges of fabric, wrap fabric around cord, and fuse in place to form flange.
4. Insert flange of welting into top and bottom of cornice where fabrics meet.

**Supplies**
- June Tailor® Deco-Wrap® No-Sew Cornice
- two coordinating fabrics
- $7/8$"w fusible web tape
- curtain rod
- two large tassels
- safety pins

**Techniques You'll Need**
- Measuring Your Window (p. 122)
- Fusing Basics (p. 72)
- Fabric Trim (p. 76)

1. Mount curtain rod inside window frame. Measure your window to determine finished width and length of balloon shade. Multiply width by $2^1/2$; add $2^1/2$" to length. Cut remaining fabric this size for shade.
2. Make a 1" single hem along bottom and side edges of shade. Fuse web tape along top edge of shade; press top edge $1^1/2$" to wrong side. Remove paper backing, refold, and fuse in place.
3. Remove curtain rod and insert into casing of shade; replace rod in window.

4. For sashes, measure length of shade; multiply by $1^1/2$. Cut two 5" wide strips of desired fabric the determined measurement and make fabric trim, following only Step 1 on page 76.
5. Thread a tassel onto each sash. Wrap each sash around shade with ends at top of shade behind rod; use safety pins to pin ends of sash together, gathering shade in window.
6. Follow manufacturer's instructions to cut cornice board as needed to fit window. Wrap with two fabrics and mount above balloon shade.

### Supplies
- June Tailor® No-Sew Shade
- two coordinating fabrics
- fusible web
- hot glue gun
- gimp trim
- $^7/_8$"w fusible web tape
- decorative rod with finials and mounting brackets
- $1^1/_2$"w wired-edged ribbon

### Techniques You'll Need
- Fusing Basics (p. 72)
- Measuring Your Window (p. 122)
- Single Hem (p. 76)

1. Follow manufacturer's instructions to cover shade with fabric. Cut a $3^3/_4$" strip of fusible web the width of shade. Fuse to wrong side of coordinating fabric; cut out. Fuse fabric strip along bottom of shade. Glue trim along seam between fabrics. Hang shade in window.
2. Follow manufacturer's instructions to hang brackets on wall above window. Place rod on brackets.

3. For swag, measure between brackets; add 24". Cut coordinating fabric 60" by determined measurement. Make a 1" single hem along edges of fabric.
4. Drape swag over brackets and rod. Wrap ribbon around swag and rod inside one bracket; tie in a bow. Repeat with remaining side of swag.

### Supplies
- 2" wide flat tension rod
- toile fabric
- $^7/_8$"w fusible web tape
- ribbon

### Techniques You'll Need
- Measuring Your Window (p. 122)
- Fusing Basics (p. 72)
- Joining Fabric Panels (p. 109)
- Matching Prints (p. 122)
- Single Hem (p. 76)

1. Mount curtain rod inside window frame. Measure your window to determine finished width and length of balloon shade. Multiply width by 2; add $2^1/_2$" to length. Cut fabric determined measurements (you may need to join two fabric panels to get a big enough piece).
2. Make a 1" single hem along bottom and side edges of shade. Fuse web tape along top edge of shade; press top edge $1^1/_2$" to wrong side. Remove paper backing and fuse in place.

3. Remove rod and insert into casing of shade; replace rod in window.
4. Without cutting, loop ribbon around valance at center to determine ribbon length. Knot ribbon at back of curtain and cut off. Cut two more pieces of ribbon the same size; loop around valance on each side and knot at back of curtain. Adjust fabric as desired.

# fringed
# OTTOMAN

*Ottomans are so diverse! They can be used as coffee tables, footstools, or extra seating. And as this one so gracefully demonstrates, they're also dramatic decorative elements.*

**TIP** When using a flea market find, test it out for stability – tighten screws, reglue, and reinforce your furniture as necessary before transforming it into a safe and useful piece.

A round wooden coffee table serves as the base for this beautiful showpiece. A generous layer of foam gives the ottoman both added height and cushiony comfort, while the soft, subtle floral pattern offers a genteel sentiment. Flowing bullion fringe evokes the notion that this is a cherished family heirloom that has been carefully preserved and passed down from generation to generation.

# layered OTTOMAN

*Lending comfort and style, ottomans are gaining in popularity. Whether your room is casual, elegant, or something in between, you can make an ottoman to suit your space.*

TIP In decorating, using odd numbers of things is more visually appealing. When mixing and matching fabrics, choose three or five. Think – "stripe, plaid, print" and "small, medium, large" on fabric design sizes.

A trio of coordinating fabrics — fanciful florals, cheery checks, and sophisticated stripes — blends beautifully to make this ottoman a real showstopper. Eyelash fringe cording and looped trim separate the various fabric layers to produce a dimensional quality.

# colorful
## OTTOMANS

*Ottomans are ideal accents for any room. And the selection of fabrics to cover them is endless, so it's a breeze to choose prints that are packed with personality.*

This pair of ottomans can be defined with one word . . . cheerful! The multi-purpose storage ottomans are covered in whimsical fabrics that add fun to functionality. An artful blend of swirls and circles plays up the lines of a square ottoman. Encircled in black ball fringe, a round footstool looks splendid in a cascade of colorful stripes topped by an eye-pleasing floral pattern.

**TIP** Use these fun ottomans for toy storage in a kid's room – they double as a child-size seat!

### Supplies
- sandpaper and tack cloth
- round wooden coffee table
- primer
- paint and paintbrush
- 6" thick foam
- fabric
- batting
- staple gun
- hot glue gun
- 6" bullion fringe
- flat decorative trim

### Techniques You'll Need
- Cutting a Circle (p. 109)
- Bonding with Glue (p. 77)

1. Sand table legs as necessary and wipe with tack cloth to remove dust.
2. Prime, then paint base.
3. Cut a piece of foam the size of the tabletop.
4. For the fabric cover, measure the diameter of the tabletop; divide the measurement in half, then add 9". Cut a circle from fabric the determined measurement.

5. Cut a piece of batting slightly smaller than the fabric piece.
6. Center the foam, then tabletop on the batting.
7. Smooth batting over foam, then staple opposite edges of the batting to the bottom of the tabletop. Continue to work on opposite sides of the tabletop and staple batting in place, smoothing it evenly around the tabletop and folding to ease in place. If necessary, trim excess batting from the bottom of the tabletop (photo 1).
8. Center the tabletop on the wrong side of the fabric, then pulling the fabric taut, repeat Step 7 to attach fabric to tabletop.
9. Glue bullion fringe around the bottom of the tabletop, then glue trim along the top of the bullion fringe (photo 2).

### Supplies
- ottoman
- three coordinating fabrics
- staple gun
- $7/8$"w fusible web tape
- craft fusible interfacing
- hot glue gun
- eyelash fringe cording with flange
- looped trim

### Techniques You'll Need
- Fusing Basics (p. 72)
- Single Hem (p. 76)
- Bonding with Glue (p. 77)

1. Wrap ottoman in fabric, gathering at corners (photo 1) and stapling along bottom edge of cushion. Trim excess fabric.
2. For each side of skirt, cut a piece of interfacing the length of the side by the measurement from floor to 1" above base of ottoman.

3. Fuse interfacing piece to wrong side of fabric; cut out fabric 1" outside edges of interfacing. Make a 1" single hem along one long edge (bottom) and both side edges of fabric piece.
4. For corner pieces to create pleated look, cut four 8" pieces of interfacing the measurement from floor to 1" above base. Repeat Step 3 to finish corner pieces.
5. Centering fabric piece on corner, staple one corner piece to each bottom corner of ottoman. Staple side pieces along bottom sides of ottoman.
6. For middle strip, measure from bottom of cushion to bottom of ottoman; add 1". Cut fabric this width and long enough to wrap around bottom of ottoman and overlap itself by 2". Make a

1" single hem along top long edge of fabric and along one end. Glue flange of cording along wrong side of top edge. With cording along top edge and overlapping fabric with hemmed end on top, glue fabric strip around bottom of ottoman.
7. Glue looped trim along bottom of fabric strip.

**Supplies**
- square storage ottoman
- acrylic paint and paintbrush
- two coordinating fabrics
- $7/8$"w fusible web tape
- hot glue gun
- staple gun
- gimp trim

**Techniques You'll Need**
- Fusing Basics (p. 72)
- Single Hem (p. 76)
- Bonding with Glue (p. 77)

1. Remove feet from ottoman; paint as desired and reattach.
2. Measure around base of ottoman; add 2". Measure height of ottoman; add 3". Cut a piece of fabric the determined measurements.
3. Make a 1" single hem on one short edge of fabric.

4. Wrap fabric around ottoman, overlapping and gluing short edges together with hemmed edge on top. Wrap fabric over top edge and glue fabric inside ottoman. Allow to dry. Pulling fabric taut, wrap fabric to bottom of ottoman and staple in place. Trim excess fabric.
5. Glue gimp trim along raw edge of fabric inside ottoman.
6. To cover lid piece, measure from bottom of lid, up one side, across top, and down remaining side; add 2". Cut a square of fabric this size.
7. Place lid on wrong side of fabric. Folding at corners, pull fabric taut to bottom of lid and staple in place along bottom edge (photo 1).

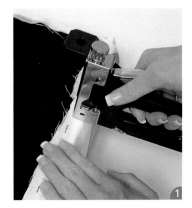

**TIP** In different fabrics, these ottomans would be great for storage in any room, such as a bathroom to hide your hair dryer and curling iron.

**Supplies**
- round storage ottoman
- acrylic paint and paintbrush
- two coordinating fabrics
- $7/8$"w fusible web tape
- hot glue gun
- staple gun
- gimp trim
- ball fringe
- craft glue

**Techniques You'll Need**
- Fusing Basics (p. 72)
- Single Hem (p. 76)
- Bonding with Glue (p. 77)

*Use hot glue for all gluing unless otherwise indicated.*

1. Remove feet from ottoman; paint as desired and reattach.

2. Measure around base of ottoman; add 2". Measure height of ottoman; add 3". Cut a piece of fabric the determined measurements.
3. Make a 1" single hem on one short edge of fabric.
4. Wrap fabric around ottoman, overlapping and gluing short edges together with hemmed edge on top. Wrap fabric over top edge and glue fabric inside ottoman. Allow to dry. Pulling fabric taut, wrap fabric to bottom of ottoman and staple in place. Trim excess fabric.
5. Glue gimp trim along raw edge of fabric inside ottoman. Glue ball fringe 1" from top edge around outside of ottoman.

6. To cover lid piece, draw around lid on wrong side of coordinating fabric. Cut out 3" outside drawn lines. Wrap fabric around lid and adhere by gluing or stapling. If underside of lid has an attached board, use craft glue and gently poke fabric beneath board with the back edge of a butter knife (photo 1).

# selecting fabrics

1. Start with an "inspiration" fabric that provides the color palette and sets the decorating mood and theme.

2. Mix in a small plaid or a solid with some textural interest as a second fabric.

3. Choose a medium-sized print or a fabric inspired by one of the colors in your inspirational fabric.

When choosing fabric, remember to select fabric that is appropriate for your project. For instance, don't use silk to cover a chair seat if you'll be sitting in it every day.

Also, you're not limited to a certain number of fabric patterns. Start with three different patterns, but feel free to mix in several others to add small dashes of color or pattern to your décor.

Trims are the "icing on the cake" — your projects' crowing glory. Splurge a bit on your trims to add that extra-special touch.

TROPICAL TREASURE

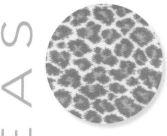

The inspiration fabric is a bold print with tropical motifs.

The accent fabric features a small print in a color that "jumps."

A neutral, diagonal "plaid" with palm trees further enhances the tropical theme.

The trims are very textured, from jute braid to beaded fringe.

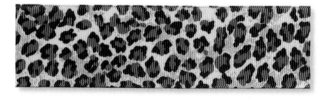

**T I M E L E S S   T E A   R O O M**

A traditional toile provides the color palette, and its large print draws in the eye.

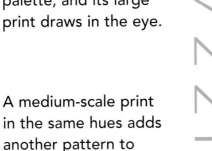

A medium-scale print in the same hues adds another pattern to the mix.

A small plaid design adds visual interest while staying in the two-tone palette established by the toile.

The trims are very traditional — tasseled fringe, brushed fringe, and looped fringe.

**F R U I T   P U N C H   P I Z Z A Z**

The bright color and swirled pattern of the inspiration fabric sets a whimsical mood.

Polka dots in a different color, yet same intensity, continue the playful theme.

Black and white fabric adds contrast, and even the stripes have a whimsical quality.

The trims are bold and include jumbo rick-rack and hot pink ball fringe for a fanciful touch.

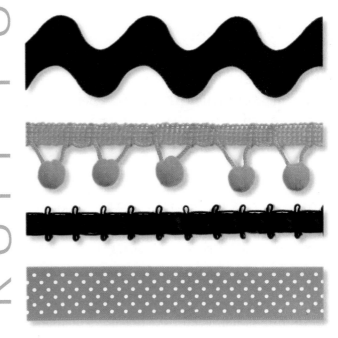

137

**R E T R E A T**

The inspiration fabric is a plaid silk with many color variations in the same tones.

Microsuede in a solid color adds rich texture and complements the modern look.

Tone-on-tone silk damask lends sophisticated elegance to the room.

**O A S I S**

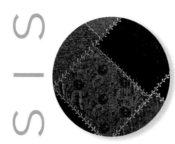

The inspiration fabric is a patchwork brocade in rich jewel tones with gold metallic accents.

A quilted fabric in a deep garnet color provides lavish texture.

The gold metallic fabric adds eye-catching shine.

**M O D E R N**

The trims are limited in order to achieve a sleek design. The microsuede fabric was cut into 1" strips to create a ribbon for the lampshades.

**M O R O C C A N**

The trims are an elegant mix of metallic flat braids, dangling beads, and woven brocade.

## COTTAGE

The inspiration fabric is a scenic floral print with country motifs.

A small, coordinating print is ideal for projects such as the lampshades.

The plaid fabric repeats the color palette choices and provides a traditional "anchor."

## CASUAL

The trims are varied, but all are "non-fussy" to create a casual feel.

## MÉLANGE

The inspiration fabric is a richly toned harlequin design.

The large toile print plays up the "French" theme.

A small print repeats the color tone choices but adds a bit of fun to the overall look.

## PARISIAN

The trims stay in the rich two-tone palette established by the inspiration fabric.

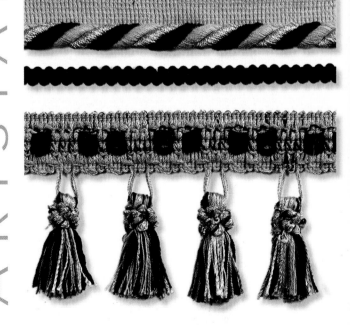

# decorative trims

Choose decorative trim(s) to complete a project...layering trims also adds dimension and interest. Using trims can also cover staples, seams, and flaws.

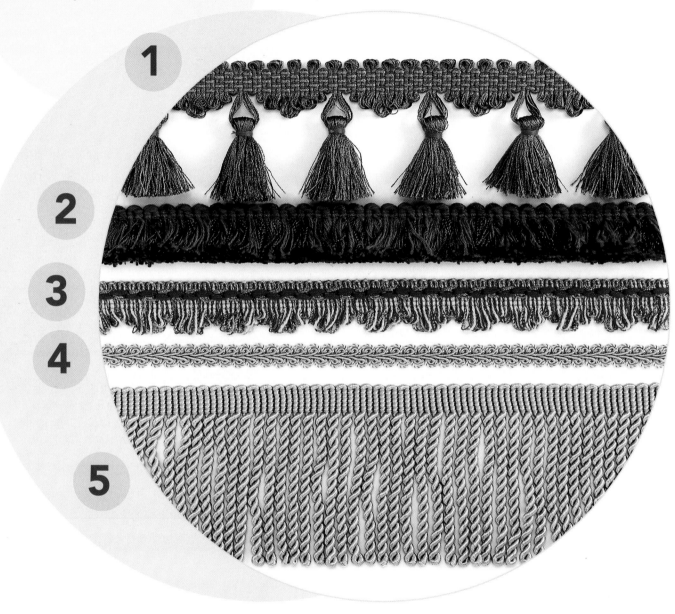

**1.** Tassel fringe
**2.** Cut or brushed fringe
**3.** Loop fringe with decorative header braid
**4.** Flat gimp trim
**5.** Bullion fringe

**TIP** When adding trim(s) to your project, always start and stop with the ends at an inconspicuous place. You can also cover trim ends with another decorative element, like a button, bow, or tassel.

1. Twisted cord
2. Twisted cord with flange
3. Ostrich cord with flange
4. Flat woven brocade ribbon
5. Beaded trim with satin ribbon flange
6. Beaded trim with twill tape flange

**TIP** When using trim, mitering the corners by gently bending the trim around the corners gives a more finished look to your project.

# what does it mean?

appliqué – the process of attaching one or more small pieces of fabric to a larger piece of fabric

batting – cotton or polyester padding used for quilting and upholstery; available in various weights and thicknesses (loft)

bias – a line diagonal to the lengthwise and crosswise grains of a woven fabric; true bias is at a 45° angle to the selvages; the direction in which the fabric has the most stretch or give

brocade – heavy fabric with a raised design

burlap – loosely-woven fabric made from course thread

chenille – fabric woven with chenille cord, creating a textured surface formed by differing yarn piles

cutting mat – protects the work surface when cutting fabric or other flat items; most are self-healing (can cut on them repeatedly without cutting through the mat)

damask – heavy-weight fabric with a reversible pattern woven into it

fabric, right side and wrong side – the front or top of the fabric is the right side, generally the brighter, more colorful side; printed fabrics and fabrics with a finish have a definite right side and wrong side

fabric glue – non-water soluble, washable glue specifically made for fabric

flange – woven or ribbon strip attached to tassel trims, beaded trims, and cording; used to attach the trim or cord to another item

fuse – to join two surfaces by melting the adhesive in a fusible product with an iron

fusible, iron-on – any product that includes an adhesive that is activated by heating with an iron

gimp, gimp trim – thickly woven flat braid

hot glue – sticks of adhesive that are melted in an electric glue gun; provides a strong, long-lasting bond in items that will not be washed or dry cleaned

mitered corner – a corner where fabric or trim is cut or folded to meet at a 45° angle

muslin – inexpensive light to medium weight cotton

paper-backed fusible web – a fusible adhesive with a protective paper or silicone backing that that is activated by heating with an iron; available in sheets or by the yard

paper-backed fusible web tape – a fusible adhesive with a protective paper or silicone backing that is activated by heating with an iron; available in precut widths on rolls

polyester fiberfill – loose polyester fibers; used to stuff pillows and such

press cloth, pressing cloth – any lint-free clean cloth large enough to cover the area being pressed; keeps the bottom of your iron clean when fusing; muslin makes a good press cloth

pressing – a lifting and lowering motion of the iron used to set seams and to remove wrinkles without stretching or distorting the fabric; press, rather than iron, all seams when finished

puddled hem – the raw bottom edge of a fabric that is turned under (rather than hemmed) which allows the fabric to form a "puddle" on the floor; adds fullness to a table skirt or window dressing

raw edge – the unfinished cut side of fabric

repeat – the space (width and height) occupied by one completed pattern on fabric

rotary cutter – a fabric cutting tool with a circular blade that can cut through several layers of fabric at once; best used with a thick, clear plastic ruler as a cutting guide and a cutting mat

running stitch – a quick and easy handstitch used to sew fabric pieces together

seam – the meeting of two pieces of fabric held together with stitching or adhesive

seam allowance – the margin of fabric between the seam and the raw edge

selvage – finished outer edge on each side of purchased fabric

sheer – very light-weight, transparent fabric

spray adhesive – adhesive that comes in an aerosol spray can; dries quickly and forms a strong bond

toile – monotone or two-color fabric with pastoral scenes printed on it

# WHERE can YOU FIND IT?

## Timeless Tea Room
pages 18 – 25

*"Showcase"huck towel*
Charles Craft
910-844-3521
charlescraft.com

## Fruit Punch Pizzazz
pages 26 – 35

*velvet ribbon*
Midori Ribbon™
800-659-3049
midoriribbon.com

*ball trim*
Hollywood Trims™
Prym-Dritz Corporation
800-845-4948
dritz.com

## Casual Cottage
pages 52 – 61

*ribbon roses*
Offray®
800-344-5533
offray.com

## Pillows
pages 78 – 91

*Deco-Wrap® No-Sew Pillows*
June Tailor®
800-844-5400
junetailor.com

## Windows
pages 112 – 127

*Deco-Wrap® No-Sew Cornice*
June Tailor®
previously noted

*Deco-Wrap® No-Sew Valance*
June Tailor®
previously noted

## Ottomans
pages 128 –135

*bullion fringe*
Conso®
800-845-2431
conso.com

*ball fringe*
Hollywood Trims™
Prym-Dritz Corporation
previously noted

## Fusible Products
The following brands
of fusibles were used
throughout the book.

Steam-A-Seam®
Iron-On Fusible Web
The Warm™ Company
800-234-9276
warmcompany.com

Craft-Fuse™
Wonder-Under®
Pellon®
800-223-5275
pellonideas.com

HeatnBond®
Iron-On Adhesive
Iron-On Vinyl
Therm O Web
847-520-5200
thermoweb.com

# THANK YOU

Location Photographers: Larry Pennington and Ken West
Freelance Photostylist: Christy Tiano Myers

We would also like to extend a warm thank you to the generous people who allowed us to photograph in their homes and business:

- Randy Breece
- Lange Cheek
- Boyd and Chrissy Chitwood
- Shirley Held
- Lindsey Huckabay
- Janna Laughlin
- Ellison Poe
- Jana Spencer
- Leighton Weeks
- Amy Williams
- Westside Lofts

1/05